Acclaim for

EVERYTHING I KNOW ABOUT
BUSINESS

I LEARNED FROM THE
GRATEFUL DEAD

"In their early days, the Dead's extreme fondness for idiosyncrasy earned them a reputation as business naifs. But irony of ironies, by persevering with policies rejected by their 'smarter' brethren, they ended up as a stunning business success story. The best part was that they succeeded *because* of, not despite, those decisions. Barry Barnes's EVERYTHING I KNOW tells you how they did it."

—Dennis McNally, Grateful Dead
biographer and author of *A Long Strange
Trip: The Inside History of the Grateful Dead*

"In a culture that has come to regard humanity as a customer base and nothing else, we who followed and did business with the Grateful Dead have done our best to behave as a community, with friendship and mutual comfort as default objectives and values. Barry Barnes knows this and explains it warmly, concisely, and convincingly."

—David Gans, musician, radio producer,
music producer, author, Deadhead

EVERYTHING
I KNOW ABOUT
BUSINESS
I LEARNED FROM THE
GRATEFUL
DEAD

THE TEN MOST INNOVATIVE LESSONS
FROM A LONG, STRANGE TRIP

BARRY BARNES, PhD
WITH A FOREWORD BY JOHN PERRY BARLOW

**BUSINESS
PLUS**

NEW YORK   BOSTON

Business Plus
Hachette Book Group
237 Park Avenue
New York, NY 10017
www.HachetteBookGroup.com

Business Plus is an imprint of Grand Central Publishing.
The Business Plus name and logo are trademarks of Hachette Book Group, Inc.

The Hachette Speakers Bureau provides a wide range of authors for speaking events. To find out more, go to www.hachettespeakersbureau.com or call (866) 376-6591.

The publisher is not responsible for websites (or their content) that are not owned by the publisher.

Printed in the United States of America

First Edition: November 2011

10 9 8 7 6 5 4 3 2 1

Library of Congress Cataloging-in-Publication Data

Barnes, Barry.
   Everything I know about business I learned from the Grateful Dead : the ten most innovative lessons from a long, strange trip / Barry Barnes.—1st ed.
      p. cm.
   ISBN 978-0-446-58379-4
   1. Grateful Dead (Musical group)   2. Strategic planning.   3. Social media—Economic aspects.   4. Success in business.   I. Title.
   HD30.28.B3677 2011
   658.4'012—dc22
                                                          2011015252

This book is deadicated to Augustus Owsley "Bear" Stanley III. Without Bear's efforts and involvement, it's hard to know if there would have been a Grateful Dead or what shape the band might have taken. Owsley produced the purest, finest LSD used in the Bay Area and in the Acid Tests that ultimately became the model for a Grateful Dead concert. He was the band's patron and supported them in the early years. And he was the soundman who helped and inspired the band to create the world's finest sound system. He passed away in March 2011.

Acknowledgments

Over the years, I've read many books and their many "acknowledgments." Typically I've glanced at the acknowledgments, but more often than not, I've simply skipped them, because I didn't appreciate their importance or value. But now that I've written my own book, the need for an acknowledgments section is clear: this book wouldn't be in your hands without the many contributions of the folks I'm going to acknowledge and thank here. Some have made a nearly lifelong contribution, others a more recent but significant contribution, and I'm very grateful to all of them and the countless others who aren't mentioned here by name.

So let me start with Mark Essig, my personal editor. Mark took my writings on the Dead's approaches to an improvisational business model—shared leadership, customer service, teamwork, core values, do-it-yourself business innovation, and nurturing the Deadhead culture—and helped me present them in a coherent, smooth-flowing, and engaging story. He helped me shape the lessons in a way I couldn't have by myself.

Next to thank and acknowledge is John Perry Barlow, who was on the scene with the Dead before I was even a serious listener. He was a Dead lyricist, road manager, and rancher who helped bring a cowboy culture to the early Dead scene, and who went on to cofound the Electronic Frontier Foundation, which established the early rules of the Internet game to keep the Web free and wide open. His foreword to this book is greatly appreciated because it complements and amplifies many of the Grateful Dead lessons I present.

Sara Weiss at Grand Central Publishing has been a wonderful collaborator throughout the book process and overlooked my lack of knowledge about writing and publishing while helping me fine-tune the book to be sure it would be the best it could possibly be.

Howard Yoon, my agent, helped me work my way through the publishing labyrinth and connected me to Grand Central Publishing and to Mark Essig. He held my hand in the early stages, and he and his partner, Gail Ross, worked hard to keep the process moving forward.

Nicholas Meriwether, the Grateful Dead archivist at the University of California, Santa Cruz, McHenry Library, has been a remarkable source of inspiration and support for more than a dozen years. Nick led by example with a Grateful Dead book of his own, *All Graceful*

Instruments, and four volumes of the *Dead Letters* journal. He's kept after me to tell the business side of the Grateful Dead story, and I'm pleased to finally be able to have finished it.

Josh Green is responsible for lighting the fire in me that started me writing this book. He interviewed me in July 2009 for an article he wrote in *The Atlantic* titled, "Management Secrets of the Grateful Dead." After the interview, I knew it was time to finally sit down and write, so I began in earnest then. When his article was published in March 2010, it was clear there was tremendous interest in the topic.

Rob Weiner, founder of the annual Grateful Dead Caucus of Dead scholars, has been another source of ongoing support and inspiration, and has led the way by authoring three Grateful Dead books himself. I'm grateful for his assistance with documents, citations, and moral support, and for getting me started on the path to this book.

David Gans is a wonderful friend who was reticent about my book when I first began talking with him about it in 1998. But his knowledge and contributions over the years have made a big difference in this book.

Alan Trist first met Jerry Garcia in 1960 and worked for the Dead organization for many years, and still runs Ice Nine Publishing. His remarkable insight into the operation of the Dead organization, his willingness to discuss how things really worked, and his internal document "A Balanced Objective" were all invaluable for helping me understand how the business operated, and helping me tell the story.

Dennis McNally provided tremendous detail on the inner workings of the Dead organization and was extremely helpful whenever I reached out to him.

Rebecca Adams is a pioneer in the academic world for taking the risk to legitimize the study of the Grateful Dead. She generously shared her unpublished manuscript on Deadhead culture and has long been a supporter of my Dead business research.

Stan Spector and Jim Tuedio have been involved in the Grateful Dead Caucus of Dead Scholars for many years and were kind enough to publish my essay on strategic improvisation in their book *The Grateful Dead in Concert: Essays on Live Improvisation.*

Art Weinstein is a friend and colleague who shares my passion for music and was the first to publish my work on the Grateful Dead. My case study on customer service appears in his book *Superior Customer Value in the New Economy: Concepts, Cases, and Applications.*

Randy Pohlman, the dean emeritus of the Huizenga School, not only supported my business research on the Dead but encouraged it as well. That's hard to find in the academic world.

My brother, Chuc Barnes, has helped me in countless ways throughout my life, including giving me a life-changing writing lesson when I was in eighth grade. He has shared my passion for the Grateful Dead and has always provided tremendous support for my research and writing.

This book would not have been possible without the ongoing support and love I've received from my wonderful wife, Chris. She allowed me to take her to 150 Dead concerts, put up with my taping of the shows, accepted my continual listening to concert recordings, and has always encouraged my writing efforts.

Many others have helped shape this book and contributed to it in many different ways. They include David Parker, Jan Simmons, Dan Healy, Peter McQuaid, Jerilyn Lee Brandelius, Traci Fordham, Kitty Preziosi, Kenneth Mackenzie, Bill Johnson, Glenn Rifkin, Wayne Huizenga, Blair Jackson, David Dodd, and Mary Eisenhart.

Finally, I must thank Jerry, Phil, Bobby, Billy, Pigpen, Mickey, Brent, and Vince. These guys are the best! They created a remarkable musical group that spawned an unrivaled following of Deadheads, created a new business model for the music industry, and set an example for an alternative approach to business in general. Long live the Dead!

Contents

Foreword

*Everything I Know About Business
I Learned from the Grateful Dead*

John Perry Barlow

What a long, strange trip it's been...
—Grateful Dead, "Truckin'"

No shit.

The real marvel is that the Grateful Dead made this declaration back in 1969. Considering all that went down during the four very weird decades since then, it becomes obvious that we[1] didn't begin to know the meaning of

---

[1] Throughout this foreword, you will find me using the first-person plural pronoun when referring to the Grateful Dead. I have misgivings about that, since not only was I never onstage with a guitar, but I was certainly, after Hunter, the "junior varsity" songwriter. Moreover, I neither lived in California nor had to work on tour (aside from a brief stint as the road manager in 1980), so I often felt like an outsider. But even so, the fact remains that I was probably the only outsider who was also an insider. Thus, I am part of "we..."

"long" *or* "strange" at that point. (We did, however, have a pretty firm grasp of the meaning of "trip" ...)

I have been intimately involved with the assembly of phenomena generally referred to as the Grateful Dead since my dewy youth forty-four years ago, during which time my sense of irony has been honed and burnished to a high sheen by the operation of something called *enantiodromia*, the process by which everything is continually becoming its opposite. According to Heraclitus, this is the fundamental operating principle of the universe, and, whether that's true or not, it has certainly been visibly in evidence around the Grateful Dead, about whom the opposite of any accurate statement one might make was also generally true—or at least became so eventually.

Consider, for example, that I'm now writing a foreword to a book proposing that this anarchic, antimaterialistic, profligate, reckless, besotted, impractical, idealistic, spontaneity-obsessed, dynamically careless, and acid-addled mob added up to a sharp business organization. This doesn't surprise me as it would someone of a more linear view. It's ironic, sure, but what isn't?

When I first heard of this project, I thought that what was being proposed was a book about the larger dimensions of our having pioneered, however accidentally, one of the most important innovations of the information economy: viral marketing. There is much to be said on this subject, and there is much that I *have* said and written about over the last twenty years.

But, no, further discussion clarified for me that this was to be a book about how the Grateful Dead had successfully created or harnessed a broad range of strategic practices in management and business that might be emulated by other commercial organizations. This struck me as a somewhat less credible proposition.

Yes, a huge amount of money was generated—though it was mostly spent as quickly as it was made. (I remember one strange morning in 1980 when Jerry Garcia appeared on *Good Morning America*. They cut to a live shot of a particularly funky Deadhead waiting at dawn in the ticket line outside Radio City Music Hall. They asked him what he did and he said something like "I do whatever I need to so that I can make enough money to tour with the band." Cut back to the studio, where perky Joan Lunden asked Garcia what he thought about someone who spent all his money following the Grateful Dead around. Garcia, who wasn't much enjoying being up at that hour, growled, "What do you think *we* do?")

This was essentially true at the time. Though still some years away from the mega-success that hit in 1987, torrents of money were already passing through our vicinity. I used to say that the Grateful Dead lived a hand-to-mouth existence, "but it's a big hand and a big mouth," I would add. To the extent that most would say thrift plays an important role in sound business management, we managed to get by without it. Moreover, it always seemed to me that the sometimes dizzying success of the

Grateful Dead had much to do with a number of happy accidents that were the business equivalent of staggering into the river and coming out with a pocketful of fish.

I don't mean to diminish the quality of our core product. The music of the Grateful Dead was, on a good night, as marvelous as any sound that has ever delighted the human ear (though it was also true that on a bad night, it was, as a well-known musician once muttered to me during a particularly incomprehensible passage through "space," like "the Special Olympics of rock 'n' roll").

In Wyoming we like to say that even a turkey can fly in a strong enough wind, and, however ungainly its commercial aerodynamics, it must be admitted that a mighty wind has blown around the Grateful Dead and its survivors for almost half a century. Whether that wind arose from the music or the whimsies of Fate or some crazy genius hidden in our anarchic decision-making processes, we certainly displayed a knack for sustaining it once it began to howl.

But aside from acknowledging that the music was sometimes transcendent and recognizing the critical role that the inadvertent invention of viral marketing had played in spreading that awareness, I never gave much thought to the other "secrets of our success."

Now comes this book, and I'm moved to reconsider. Even after taking into consideration that Mr. Barnes is a freely confessed Deadhead and thus in a condition that may blunt his critical capacities in our regard, he makes herein some assertions about the emergent wisdom of our mad methods that seem true to me. Viewed from his side of the proscenium and thereby abstracted from the sausage factory of their creation, he is able to see what we could not: that our commercial "policies," though improvised adaptations to a set of unprecedented conditions, actually *do* reflect some principles that might be generalized for wider corporate use, especially by those legacy companies that are struggling to find footing in an information economy.

First, of course, was the accidental brilliance of letting the audience tape the concerts. It wasn't our initial response and certainly wasn't something that Warner Bros., our record company at the time, supported. But Deadheads are a sweet and hapless lot. Nobody felt right about the baleful glances they cast our way as they and their cassette recorders were being given the bum's rush. Besides, if they actually *were* stealing something, nobody was quite sure what it was. Finally, Garcia pointed out that we weren't in it for the money, which was an easy thing to say at that point since we were hardly making any. Without precisely encouraging taping, it was decided to leave the tapers alone, unless they became irritating to other members of the audience. Which, being a meticulous lot, they eventually did. At that point, sometime in the seventies, it was decided to concentrate them in a little ghetto near the soundboard. As far as I can recall, this was the only time that taping was ever *officially* sanctioned.

But by that point, the tapers had already created something that Warner Bros. could not: a successful way to market Grateful Dead music. They spread the contagion not simply by word-of-mouth but by "hear-of-ear," endowing us eventually with a following so devoted that we could, for a time, fill any stadium in America. This was largely through the expediency of hauling the audience around with us, but the fact remained: we *could*. The fans knew, based on hearing the tapes, that every concert would be different. If they didn't hear them all, they'd be missing out. It wasn't about buying a *thing*. It was about being part of a flow. It wasn't an economy of nouns. It was an economy of verbs.

There were several benefits—not well understood at the time—that descended from this happy accident of leniency, all of which Mr. Barnes recognizes and expounds upon here.

The most important of these was that music is a product of an information economy and that an information economy is fundamentally different from a physical economy. In the latter, as Adam Smith pointed out two centuries ago, there is a set of rules based on the hard-coupled relationship between scarcity and value in the physical world. Thus, if your product is physical, it makes sense to regulate toward scarcity, as the folks at De Beers harnessed successfully by cornering most of those regions of the planet that produce diamonds. (Diamonds are actually quite common, but De Beers was able to make them scarce and thus more valuable.) The same rules apply to everything from real estate to pork bellies.

I believe that these rules do not apply to expression, where there appears to be an equally strong relationship between *familiarity* and value instead. I might have the world's largest diamond in my pocket and its enormous worth will remain the same whether or not anyone knows it's there. But the world's greatest song has no value to anyone but me as long as it remains in my head. Indeed, if I sing it to a few friends, they may love it, but it still has limited value. Only when a lot of people have heard and enjoyed it does it start to accumulate value, and even then not so much for itself but for me as its source. In this, music is more like a *service*, something that is continuously provided, rather than an *object* of commerce. The more people who become aware of the quality of that service, the more that can be economically derived from providing real-time access to its provision. Thus, every time we "gave away" a show to the tapers, we increased the value of the music that hadn't been played yet.

I wrote a piece about this for *Wired* magazine in 1994 called "The Economy of Ideas," which has been expounded on many times since, and which foreshadowed a variety of subsequent events, including Napster, the decline of the traditional record industry, and creation of what is known as Web 2.0.

The term *Web 2.0* generally refers to the idea that the audience is the product—a principle that is fundamental to the success of Facebook, Twitter, Wikipedia, and a host of others, and which the Grateful Dead began to take unwitting advantage of back in the seventies. At one point, I took an inner-city friend to a Dead concert, which he seemed to enjoy. I asked him if he would come back again and he replied, "Nah, I don't think so. Seems to me that what you guys are selling here is a sense of community, and I already have one." Which was true. Most of our fans were white suburban kids who'd grown up on television and in a culture too commercially massive to provide them with a sense of *belonging*. Heading out on tour with eighteen dollars in change, a Microbus with three working cylinders, and a sense of magical possibility inspired our fans to form the kind of necessary interdependency that shared adversity generally provides. They became a community. They liked it. Their stories of adventure and peril became a very effective recruiting tool. A lot of what we were selling them was themselves.

In addition to community, we were selling another product that is fundamental to an information economy. We were selling an authentic and unique *experience*. Of course, there is a paradox in this, since there is a huge but poorly recognized difference between information and experience, and the old media that have tried to enter the information economy fail to recognize that the information itself is not as valuable as the relationships and experiences that form around it. Furthermore, the more bombarded we are with information, particularly broadcast information, the more we long for the real stuff of life. In a sense then, the information that was the Dead's taped or recorded music became an advertisement and convening beacon for the ineffable experience of being *there* in surreal time, of being in a place where it seemed, on some nights, that God Itself would show up.

And yes, there was a religious aspect to it. That cannot be denied. Nor can it be denied that this was a fundamental element of both our commercial success and our longevity. As many saints and charlatans have learned over the years, if you want to make a lot of money, start a religion. Of course, we were not really interested in doing either of these things and when it became obvious that we were and had, we had profoundly mixed feelings about the money and a genuine horror about the religion. (Fortunately, Bob Hunter and I recognized that the most toxic aspect of religion is dogma and, while we couldn't do much about stopping twenty thousand people who were taking LSD together from experiencing the Holy Who Knows, there was a lot we could do to keep It from seeming to make dogmatic pronouncements, since these would likely be found in the lyrics, and generally his. So we avoided preaching.)

But even without dogma or our willing participation,

the mysterious cult of the Dead formed all manner of myths, rituals, and divination practices. For example, the audience became obsessively focused on the set lists, much in the same way that certain baseball fans memorize the welter of multi-decimal statistics associated with the game. Ask Deadheads what songs were played on any given night and in what order, and a disturbingly large percentage of them can tell you accurately. This was more than ordinary consumer product awareness. It became a way of finding the implicit order that grounds a chaotic world.

We didn't create the first cult product. Indeed, Mr. Barnes's former employer, John Deere, had generated an equally fixated zeal in its customers clear back in the nineteenth century and even did so by somewhat similar means: its drive to manufacture products that embedded in them the ideals of its culture resulted in a long tradition of eccentric but highly effective designs...and a following who regarded other farm equipment as, well, impure. (I was a cattle rancher for twenty years and this was certainly how I came to feel about the green machines.)

And I hardly need to mention Apple Computer in this regard. Steve Jobs has become a cult figure to a degree that makes Jerry Garcia look like a good start. Of course, unlike Garcia, Jobs hasn't resisted being cast in this role and has even injected an element of moral sanctimony into the "Cult of Mac" that would have been anathema to us.

While we were unwilling to impose our own moral views on anyone, the fact remained that the culture of the Grateful Dead actually *did* embody a lot of the giddy, open-hearted sixties values, at which it's now so fashionable to poke fun. As an organizational whole, we went on standing for them even after the darker forces of sex, drugs, and rock 'n' roll had taken some of the gleam from our eyes. While many would claim that it's wildly impractical to run a business on the principle that "what goes around comes around," I would say that we pretty much did that for forty years, and if you add it all up, we came out way ahead.

The faith we extended to our fans was consistently rewarded. For example, when it became obvious that we were going to allow taping, we did ask the audience not to make any commercial use of the tapes. And even though there were certain concerts of which a good tape was as valuable as a one-of-a-kind baseball card, I never saw anyone selling tapes. The Deadheads had a hot barter economy in such things, but it was scrupulously self-regulatory. Indeed, it seems that just about every time we showed faith in our "market," it was rewarded.

Consider the way we ran our philanthropic arm, the Rex Foundation. When we established it in 1983, the original board—the band members, the songwriters, and folks like Bill Walton, Bill Graham, and Mountain Girl Garcia—shared with its "executive director," Danny Rifkin, a horror of the organizational nest-feathering that

is the nearly universal disease of the nonprofit world. So
we set out to make a foundation that was designed along
much leaner than normal lines. Our records fit in a box
in the trunk of Rifkin's car.

Although there were some years in which we generated—
with especially dedicated concert runs—and gave away
over a million dollars, we didn't accept grant propos-
als. Instead, each board member would identify worthy
little machete-and-loincloth nonprofits—ranging from
needle exchanges to composers of "difficult" music—
who were too busy doing good to spend a lot of time
asking for money. At board meetings we'd agree to surprise these unsuspecting saints with donations of anywhere from five thousand to twenty-five thousand bucks
and we didn't require that they report on what they
did with the money. As an organizational system, this
sounds wholly irresponsible. Yet it worked amazingly
well. Years after Rex started giving away money in this
reckless fashion, we checked back on the original recipients and found that most of them, barely functional
when we encountered them, had gone on to do great and
lasting work.

Even though I continue to believe that I have never
been around a philanthropic foundation that operated
with anything like the efficiency and effectiveness of
Rex, it never occurred to me to suggest that anyone else
try it. It simply required too much faith in everybody—
from the fans, who happily paid for tickets to Rex shows

(rather than relying on "miracles" to somehow get them in) to the board members whose whims were trusted to identify deserving recipients, to the recipients themselves, who were never asked to prove in detail what they'd done with the money.

But we are at a particularly cynical moment in the history of American business. The trust we've traditionally had in our engines of commerce has taken a severe beating over the last decade. The benign organizational principles that reigned for a long golden time after the Second World War have become more predatory. Perhaps it's time to give trust a chance.

Also, because of the Internet, we are moving into an economic epoch the fundamental laws of which are still being promulgated. Maybe it actually *is* becoming practical to create an environment of common purpose with one's customers, employees, and stakeholders. Not just to talk about it, as every company does, but to do it. Our existing regulatory methods, to the extent they haven't been gutted, no longer seem effective against unrestrained greed. Perhaps in the absence of effective laws, we have no choice but to return to shared ethical principles and an enlightened sense of the common good to guide us into the future.

As I've said, there was a lot about the Grateful Dead in its entire context that felt more than a little like a religion. It certainly felt like a community with a common set of generally unspoken beliefs to guide its decisions. On a good day, it felt like being on a mission from God. What-ever uneasiness one might rightfully feel about turning a business into a holy mission, you can't deny that when it works, it works. And besides, it feels good.

There was a lot that worked for the Grateful Dead. Indeed, upon examination, it becomes obvious that Mr. Barnes is on to more here than I first suspected. After reading this book, I'm forced to admit that a lot of the characteristics Barnes identifies as being central to our business style are accurately identified and may actually be useful now to different organizations as they confront the puzzling present and the even more confounding future.

He notes, for example, that we had a practice of "stra-tegic improvisation," which is to say that we made our business as we made our music, with a lot of what might be called "just-in-time planning." Back in the days when history moved at a slower, more predictable pace, most business schools would have said this was just sloppy and foolish. But these are very chaotic times. Everyone is in a state of what Toffler called "future shock." As much as twenty years ago, forward-looking business thinkers, such as Tom Peters, were extolling the virtues of "ready, fire, aim" policies as a means of dancing with the weird commercial music of those frothy times. Now almost everyone has to be ready at a moment's notice for star-tling new developments.

Also, we had a creative process in which the audience played a fundamental role. We used to say that we didn't write Grateful Dead songs, we *grew* them, and we did so in a field of dense interaction with the audience. The Grateful Dead was certainly one of very few successful bands who practiced and worked up new material before a live audience. And the result was that the fans had a justified sense of ownership and participation in the material. They *were* us in some essential way. We were all in it together and they knew that. This is precisely the sort of quality that one must optimize for in Web 2.0 economics.

The fans were also pioneers in the use of social networks. When I first got online back in 1985, it was because I wanted to study the culture of the Deadheads, who had beaten me there by a couple of years and had set up lively communities on USENET and a legendary computer bulletin board called The WELL (short for Whole Earth 'Lectronic Link). By the 1990s many of the social forms that characterize Facebook and Twitter had already been in seasoned use by Deadheads.

Our emphasis on decision by consensus that had to include just about *everybody* seemed like a very clumsy tool at the time but, in the process, we were doing a lot of the early work in designing the "flat" organizations that have become far more common in recent years and include major successes such as Apple.

Hell, I guess Barnes is right about a lot of business advantages we developed without expecting them to provide much leverage. They worked. We actually *did* do well by doing good. We stayed right at the edge of technological possibility, mostly because we enjoyed the challenge and thought it was fun to try crazy new things. We created the most fiercely, one might even say helplessly, loyal customers any business ever had. We learned how to learn as a culture.

Yep. Strange indeed it is to say, but one actually *can* learn a lot about business from the Grateful Dead.

EVERYTHING
I KNOW ABOUT
BUSINESS
I LEARNED FROM THE
GRATEFUL
DEAD

Prologue

The Business Genius of the Grateful Dead

In 1969, while working for IBM, I listened to my first Grateful Dead album. I didn't much like it. About five years later I opened a record shop, Barry's Record Rack, in Kansas City, and also became a DJ on an alternative rock station. At the insistence of some of my listeners and customers, I began to spin Dead albums more often, and then went to my first show, in Des Moines, Iowa, in 1974. I could appreciate the band more, but I still didn't really get it. As Jerry Garcia, the Dead's lead guitarist and spiritual leader, once put it, "The Grateful Dead is a lot like licorice. Some people like licorice and some people don't. But the people who like it *really* like licorice." Over the next few years I developed a taste for Grateful

Dead licorice and began to really like it. I went to shows when the band came through Kansas City, and soon I started making short trips around the country to see two or three shows at a time. I even became a "taper," recording shows surreptitiously—it was still officially unsanctioned at the time—and trading them with other fans around the country.

By the early 1980s, I had started working for John Deere, and my commitment to the band was growing. Despite stereotypes of the band's fans as dropped-out hippies, the Dead have always had many fans in the business world, people who were as comfortable in a suit and tie as they were in tie-dye. Even so, I saw the Dead and my corporate job as two distinct parts of my life. The band, though, had one more major surprise in store for me. While watching the Grateful Dead play at the Greek Theatre in Berkeley, California, in 1985, I came to a realization: My two personae, Deadhead and businessman, weren't terribly different after all. It suddenly became clear to me that the Grateful Dead had some important lessons to teach the business world.

That realization changed my life. Tourheads, a small group of fanatical Dead fans, were famous for quitting their jobs and following the Dead for an entire tour. I decided to do something similar: having worked for companies such as IBM and John Deere for two decades, I quit my corporate job to start a serious study of the business legacy of the Grateful Dead. I earned an MBA and a PhD, using the Dead as a case study in organizational change, then began a career teaching and consulting, always with the Dead at the center of my thoughts. I read all the books and articles on the Dead, interviewed members of the organization, and, of course, kept going to shows (194 in all, but who's counting?). This book reveals the lessons I learned along the way.

When I tell people I study the business of the Grateful Dead, I sometimes get puzzled looks. It's true that for much of their careers the members of the Dead were anticorporate and seemed downright allergic to making sensible business decisions. Phil Lesh, the band's bassist, summed it up this way: "You could run an analysis of this business and drive an ordinary consultant berserk with the contradictions and waste in it."

Yet despite all that, it worked. Somehow it worked. The Grateful Dead managed to become one of the longest-lived, most beloved, and top-grossing acts of the late twentieth century. Founded in 1965, the band survived for thirty years and played a total of more than 2,300 shows, nearly all with the same core group of musicians: lead guitarist Jerry Garcia, bassist Phil Lesh, guitarist Bob Weir, and the two drummers, Bill Kreutzmann and Mickey Hart. On the strength of their brilliant live performances, they built an audience and added new fans slowly but steadily, all without the benefit of advertising or much radio airplay. In 1987, when their album *In the Dark* went platinum and "Touch of Grey" hit number nine on the charts, the band's career went from moderately successful to stratospheric. They became the top touring act in the country, grossing tens of millions of dollars a year, and their merchandising branch, which sold everything from T-shirts to golf balls, became the envy of the rock world. Even now, sixteen years after breaking up, the Grateful Dead remains a formidable business empire.

How did they do it?

Not by following a solid business plan.

"It's not possible for the Grateful Dead to have a business plan," Lesh once explained. "We don't even plan the music." And that, precisely, is the point. The Dead were brilliant improvisers, finding musical success in constant change and relentless variation. Those same skills lay at the root of their business success. In all of their business dealings, they adopted a strategy I call strategic improvisation—blending planning and doing while staying alert, alive to fluid situations.

By implementing a loose management style, long on flexibility and short on structure, the Dead pioneered practices and strategies that would subsequently be embraced by corporate America. They created a horizontally managed organization with shared leadership, recognizing that decentralized decision making motivated employees to produce great work and remain loyal. They adopted, long before it became trendy, a socially conscious business model focused not only on profit but also on doing good. They placed an enormous value on customer service, and understood that keeping customers happy led to greater profitability. Long before "viral marketing" became a catchphrase in the late 1990s, the Dead essentially invented the practice by allowing fans to tape live shows and share the recordings with one another. You might even say the Dead understood the world of the Internet before the Internet existed: they helped nurture a "virtual community," the Deadheads, dispersed geographically yet deeply committed to one another; they created an interactive relationship with their fans/customers, soliciting feedback and acting upon it; and they pioneered the concept of "free," giving away their content in one form and making money on it in other ways.

Members of the band might laugh at this list of accolades. Jerry and the boys never set out to be great businessmen and never considered themselves as such. In fact, they didn't much care about the business side of things, so long as it allowed them to keep playing music and making their fans happy. Their suspicions of the business world, in fact, turned out to be one of their greatest advantages, as they tossed out received wisdom and reinvented what it meant to run an organization. Throughout all their ups and downs, they remained committed to improvisation and innovation, and they were never satisfied unless they were constantly reinventing themselves, their music, and their business. In today's business climate, beset by crisis and continual change, what lesson could be more important?

1

Master Strategic Improvisation

How the Dead Learned to Plan and Act at the Same Time

Most rock bands play predetermined arrangements of their music, and they practice obsessively to achieve their desired result: the ability to play note-perfect versions of their songs. The Grateful Dead, however, weren't interested in achieving perfection and then repeating themselves. They prided themselves on never playing the same song the same way twice. "The whole thing with the Grateful Dead is a challenge to get something new happening, even when you don't...feel anything new lurking around the corner," guitarist Bob Weir once said. When they rehearsed, they weren't so much learning the songs as learning one another—each came to know the intricacies of the others' playing styles, their quirks, their strengths and weaknesses, their good and bad habits. They were challenging one another to make it new.

Improvisation is a useful skill for anyone working in an organization, whether it is a band or a major corporation. Since the 1980s, business theorists have proffered a variety of techniques intended to improve organizational flexibility and deliver better goods and services—such as Total Quality Management (enlisting every employee in the commitment to constant quality improvement) and Six Sigma (reducing the number of defects in manufacturing and business processes). Although each of these strategies made some important contributions, none seemed up to the challenge of meeting the constantly changing world of business. Given the chronic uncertainty in economic, political, and cultural climates, sometimes it's surprising that companies bother to make strategic plans at all. Planning is still vital, of course, but what today's businesses need is a new, more flexible approach to executing strategic plans.

The business theorist and jazz musician Frank Barrett has written that musicians who improvise "do what managers find themselves doing: fabricating and inventing novel responses without a pre-scripted plan and without certainty of outcomes; discovering the future that their action creates as it unfolds." No matter how strong your strategic plan is, running an organization involves making an endless series of adjustments, responding both to major crises and to the million small changes that constitute daily life. Fluid situations demand improvisation, the simultaneous blending of planning and doing. It's a concept best described as "strategic improvisation."

Strategic improvisation is the process of continually aligning spur-of-the-moment actions with long-term direction. It is solving problems innovatively by using only the resources at hand. It involves responding immediately to changing conditions while keeping the organization pointed in the right strategic direction. Requiring skill and experience, it's much more than simply flying by the seat of your pants—it's like doing major repairs on a 747 at thirty-five thousand feet in the air.

The Grateful Dead were masters of improvisation, not only in their music but also in the way they ran their business. They didn't like the mainstream business world, and they especially didn't like the way the music business was organized. But it's not as if there was an alternate model they could follow, so instead they invented one. In a sense, this entire book is a study in how the Dead improvised a new way of doing business, tossing out the conventional wisdom and creating—in fits and starts, with many costly mistakes—a new, more humane, and more profitable way of operating in the cutthroat world of entertainment.

> **Grateful Dead Business Lesson 1:** Strategic improvisation—the ability to plan, act, and make adjustments in real time—is the key to running a great organization.

The Roots of Improvisation

What is musical improvisation? For any piece of music, there will be variation depending on the performer and the performance. You might call this "interpretation." Improvisation simply takes the process of interpretation to its limits. There are still signposts—lyrics, chord progressions, rhythms, melodies—that make a certain song recognizable. But within that loose structure, the musicians have freedom to create new sounds and new patterns. Music emerges from the interaction of the players rather than from a well-defined structure in which everyone knows what comes next.

The Grateful Dead cut their teeth as a band in the fall of 1965 at a bar called the In Room in Belmont, California, between San Francisco and Palo Alto. Marvin Gaye and the Coasters played headline shows, while Garcia's band—then called the Warlocks—played five fifty-minute sets a night, six nights a week. This period might be considered the band's apprenticeship: Lesh, a virtuoso classical and jazz trumpeter, learned how to play bass; Weir, barely out of high school, polished his rudimentary guitar skills; Garcia set aside his beloved bluegrass and began to rock. There were dozens of bands in the region that had flipped out for the Rolling Stones and the Beatles, learned to play covers, wrote a few derivative originals, and found audiences in bars or at high school dances. In 1965, Garcia and the boys were not unlike those bands: they played louder and weirder, but mostly they played other people's songs in fairly conventional ways.

This soon changed, partly out of simple necessity: the band didn't know enough songs to fill their five sets a night, so they stretched out the songs they did know to fill the time. From this crude time-filling technique, musical genius was born. The band members don't recall ever discussing the possibility of improvising—they just started slowly, and soon ran with it. Garcia took the lead, drawing on his experience playing bluegrass. He recalled, in particular, the influence of the Kentucky Colonels and their great improvisational fiddler, Scotty Stoneman. Phil Lesh offered guidance in improvisation from a very different background—avant-garde jazz, especially the work of the brilliant jazz saxophonist John Coltrane, whom Lesh had seen in San Francisco clubs in the late 1950s.

As the band continued to play their grueling sets at the In Room, they noticed that the trains on nearby tracks rolled by at consistent times every night. Rather than waiting for the trains to pass, or trying to drown out the noise, they chose to play along with the rumble of the trains. Within a few nights, they took that train noise, combined it with a fragment of the song "Mystic

Eyes," by Them (whose lead singer was Van Morrison), and created "Caution (Do Not Stop on Tracks)." That is the essence of improvisation: taking something unexpected and even unwelcome—the noise from a passing train, a new competitor for your business, an economic crisis—and using it to your advantage.

How to Improvise a Business Plan

Improvisation was more than a musical technique for the Dead: it was a way of life. The band, of course, never thought of their business in terms of strategic improvisation; they just did it. It's possible, though, to take a look back and see how the Dead applied the principles of musical improvisation to their business dealings.

1. Disrupt old habits:

Habits are ingrained patterns of behavior, and because they persist below the level of consciousness, they can foil the best attempts to create change. Any business seeking to improve needs to get rid of some bad habits, both at the individual and organizational levels. By definition, improvisation aims to disrupt routine by shaping each unexpected situation into something new and interesting. With group improvisation, the members of the band act as a kind of habit-interrupting support group, encouraging one another to strike out in new directions.

That very unpredictability created the band's musical and business niche. In the late 1960s, Garcia told an interviewer that the band was trying to interrupt the classic rock 'n' roll rhythm, in which the bass and drums work together as a unit, into a sound "where the rhythm is more implied and less obvious." Lesh, Garcia explained, came to the bass when he was already an accomplished trumpet player, so he sounds "utterly different than any other bass players." The Dead were trying to escape from standard rhythms and arrangements, to avoid rigid structures and to free up some space for spontaneous creativity. The great rock 'n' roll impresario Bill Graham once said, "The Grateful Dead are not only the best at what they do; they are the only ones who do what they do." They created and owned their market.

The Dead carried this disdain for old habits into their business dealings, never trusting the standard operating procedures in the music industry. Instead of counting on preexisting resources to make and market their music and their brand, they created their own. As we'll see in more detail in later chapters, the Dead started their own record company, their own merchandising company, and their own mail-order ticketing business. The old habits just didn't work for the Dead, who epitomized the famous quotation from former Intel CEO Andy Grove, "Only the paranoid survive." The Dead's paranoia, their restlessness, prompted them to continually examine their habits and change them when necessary. As Dead lyricist Robert Hunter wrote in the classic Dead song "Uncle John's Band," "When life looks like Easy Street, there is danger at your door."

2. Embrace errors:

In musical improvisation, there's an axiom: If there are no mistakes, it's a mistake. If everything you play is perfect, you're not taking enough chances. In many businesses, to make a mistake and acknowledge it can only damage your career. Ultimately, though, this hurts the business. Imagine a toddler learning to walk without falling or a sports team unable to see the value of holding practices. The best learning often comes from making a mistake and adjusting future actions in response.

The Dead would be the first to acknowledge that they made plenty of errors. When the band formed in 1965, all five of the band members were relative novices. They improved simply by playing together, practicing endlessly, and learning from their errors. The same applied to their business efforts. Sam Cutler, a tour manager for the band from 1969 until 1974, reports that in these early years the band "didn't really have any idea how to" make money. Rather than following traditional models, however, the Dead learned by doing. One of their biggest errors came in 1969, when they hired Mickey Hart's father, Lenny, as their business manager. As a former music store owner, Lenny Hart was one of the few businessmen they knew. And since he was family, they trusted him to manage the money that had just started flowing in. The next year, Lenny fled to Mexico, having stolen about $150,000 from them. They didn't press charges. Instead, they chalked it up to experience, hired more experienced and trustworthy managers, and got back to work. Dave Parker, one of those new managers, explained that the band wanted "to leave that sort of thing behind and not get into a big ugly lawsuit or anything, but to concentrate on their music." The Dead didn't waste time regretting their mistakes. Failure was the price of improvement.

3. Minimize structure, maximize flexibility:

Organizational structures and policies are created to reduce ambiguity and provide ready-made solutions and lines of communication. Despite these benefits, however, such structures can easily become rigid, inhibiting innovation, flexibility, and improvisation. The Grateful Dead preferred to minimize structure in both music and business. Their beloved song "Dark Star," for instance, was released as a single in 1968 at less than three minutes long—yet in concert it could last anywhere from fifteen to forty-five minutes. From the song's minimal structure, the band created an enormous range of flexibility.

This same minimalist approach to structure was found in their organization. While they were never a large organization, the Grateful Dead did have seventy full-time employees in 1994, their last full year as a band. Despite a rather complicated operation, they always found it easiest to operate without job titles or job descriptions. As Garcia said, "What we wanted to do was play music, and we didn't want to have to be businessmen. We didn't even want to decide; we just wanted to play....We were truly coming from an unstructured space." In 1981 the band commissioned an internal report, called "A Balanced Objective," that attempted to define the structure of the band's business enterprises. The report, however, ended up stressing not organization but flexibility. "To define the 'flexible group process' is to lose it," the report concluded. "Its value lies in the spontaneity which comes from acknowledgement of it and openness to the unknown next point of invention." Even in its business planning documents, the Dead spoke in the language of improvisation.

4. Alternate between soloing and supporting:

In improvised music, each musician must listen to the others, then fill in and assist where needed without stepping on the others' lead. What is needed, in other words, is teamwork, and that's what the Dead forged through their years of playing together. "The arrangements are almost nil," Garcia said of their style. "The intra-band collaboration is almost total." Lesh once explained how the Dead's sense of shared responsibility created their signature sound: "Since our ideal of improvisation is collective improvisation, it's necessarily going to be more detailed, more diverse, more complicated than the kind of music where it's just a solo with accompaniment." "Solo with accompaniment" relies on one star musician to be creative while everyone else backs him up—you might think of this in terms of a command-and-control form of business management, in which all of the creativity is expected to emerge from the executive suites. If we follow the Dead's model of collective improvisation, by contrast, every person in the organization is expected to share in the creative enterprise.

The Dead also alternated between soloing and supporting organizationally, anticipating the business world's shift, decades later, toward "employee empowerment" and "shared leadership." It's now recognized that employees must not only follow but also lead, drawing on their skill and training to deal with unexpected situations. Although most people considered Garcia the leader of the Dead, he rejected any notion that he held the reins of power. Instead, as we'll see, the Dead's organization was consensus-driven, with all band members holding spots on the board of directors and even the janitors having a voice at company meetings.

5. Make sense of things retrospectively:

Frank Barrett tells us that because an improvising musician "can never know for certain where the music is going, one can only make guesses and anticipate possible paths based on what has already happened, meanwhile continue playing under the assumption that whatever happened must amount to something sensible." Put another way, the burden is on the musicians to take what they've just played, build on it, and make it work in the future.

The Dead, because they didn't like to do business planning, were forced to do a lot of retrospective sense making. This is most clearly seen in their decision to allow fans to tape concerts. Conventional wisdom held that allowing taping would cut into record sales. The Dead, though, tolerated the practice, largely because they didn't want to be authoritarian. This turned out to be a wonderful decision, as the tapes were traded widely and inspired many more people to become fans. Once the Dead realized these benefits, they embraced the tapers. Although taping made little business sense at first, retrospectively the band turned it into one of their smartest business moves. As Hunter wrote in the lyrics for "Playing in the Band," "Some folks trust to reason / Others trust to might / I don't trust to nothing / But I know it come out right."

Touring for Success

The Dead's most successful improvisation was the creation of its unusual business model—one that anticipated the plan of nearly every up-and-coming band working today.

Early in 2011 the online magazine *Slate* published an article marveling at the success of the Dave Matthews Band, which appeared among the top-ten grossing musical acts of 2010. Compared to the list's other, longer-established acts, such as Bon Jovi and Roger Waters of Pink Floyd, Dave Matthews had sold a comparatively modest number of records. Instead, his band was a success due to nearly constant touring. With the rise of digital file sharing and online music services, record sales have plummeted, never to recover. Bands in the future will make money like the Dave Matthews Band, which "lives to tour, making them not just popular, but very,

very profitable." Dave Matthews toured so much that between 2000 and 2009 they sold more tickets than any other band on earth. The *Slate* article bore the headline "The Dave Matthews Band Shows How to Make Money in the Music Industry."

The Grateful Dead, however, had demonstrated that same way to make money three decades earlier; Dave Matthews simply followed their example. The Dead, though, had no such model to follow. They were improvising their strategy from scratch.

Necessity demanded this innovation. By the early 1970s, the Dead were facing tremendous financial pressure. They kept a lot of people on staff and paid them generous wages, and they also undertook costly experiments, such as starting their own record label and investing heavily in cutting-edge sound systems. Having upended rock 'n' roll habits, however, the Dead were forced to come up with something new.

The business model for most rock 'n' roll bands was to tour just after the release of an album, in order to promote its sales. Playing live was lucrative, certainly, but record sales were a band's bread and butter. The Jefferson Airplane, good friends of the Dead, sold a lot of records and did more limited touring. The Dead tried to follow this model, but it never worked. For most of its career, the Dead managed to attract big crowds to their live shows, but they never produced the record sales to match. Their improvisations on stage didn't translate onto vinyl. As Garcia explained, "We don't make money except by going out and playing music."

And play they did. Their peak touring year was 1970, when they played an astonishing 120 shows. By the 1980s they'd settled into a regular schedule: three tours a year, in March–April, June–July, and September–October. Each tour featured 17 shows and lasted three and a half weeks. In between these tours, they did limited shows in the Bay Area and elsewhere on the West Coast. This added up to a brutal 80 shows a year.

Even after their 1987 single "Touch of Grey" became their only top-ten hit, they kept up their frantic schedule. By now touring was in their blood, and they kept at it. In 1989 the band played 73 shows in 17 states and sold out nearly every show. In the recession year of 1991, when the concert business was off by 25 percent, the Dead stayed hot and became the top-grossing act in the country. In 1993 the band played 81 shows and sold more than 1.75 million tickets—which represented 99.4 percent of all available seats. In some ways, 1995, their final year of touring, was the most remarkable. Though they played only 45 shows, they grossed $33.5 million, more than all but three other bands.

For many years the Dead wished they didn't need to tour quite so much. But in business, wish and reality are often far apart. As it turned out, relentless touring was the best thing that could have happened to them. Though they griped at times, they loved touring, and, most important, it kept them in touch with their fans. Often new businesses succeed because the most passionate employees—the owners—are still working at the ground level, enjoying face-to-face contact with customers. As these businesses expand, however, the owners become disconnected from the daily working reality, and the customer experience suffers. A Grateful Dead tour, by contrast, was the equivalent of a company's top brass getting out to meet and greet customers seventy or eighty nights a year. They stayed close to the fans, and as a result the fans stayed close to them.

Beset by a crisis—the inability to make money the way rock bands usually did—the Dead stayed nimble, kept adjusting, and pioneered a revolutionary new business model.

Operating on the Edge

Bruce Hornsby, the great pianist and songwriter who played more than a hundred shows with the Dead, often encountered other musicians who couldn't understand why he wanted to play with them. "If you're not an aficionado and you hear a live tape, well, there's lots of out-of-tune singing and out-of-time playing and lots of clams [bad chords] and mistakes, and that's hard for a lot of musicians to get past." One might imagine a mainstream businessman offering the same judgments on the Dead's business practices. But Hornsby added this: "I understand that, but I also feel sorry for those people because I think they missed something that was truly great."

Improvising may lead to mistakes, but it also opens the door to greatness. Strategic improvisation is a skill that embraces mistakes as a learning opportunity rather than ignoring them or placing blame. It thrives on flexibility but withers amid rigid hierarchies. In any given situation, it encourages those with the best skills to step forward and "solo," and then to step back and "support" when the situation changes.

The Dead improvised out of choice—they knew that by living on the edge, musically speaking, they would create the best product for their listeners. When it came to their business operations, however, they had no choice but to improvise. Other organizations often find themselves in the same boat. Dramatic change is unavoidable. It's how we respond to it that matters, and many businesses fail that test.

For example, in 2010, when Toyota faced its "unintended acceleration" crisis—involving cars that surged out of control and couldn't be stopped—the company responded slowly, initially failing to take responsibility, and the brand suffered. Likewise, when BP bungled its response to the Deepwater Horizon spill, it revealed that it was technologically inept as well as tone-deaf in public relations. For the other side of the story, think back to Johnson & Johnson's response, in the fall of 1981, to the criminal tampering with Tylenol capsules that left seven dead in Chicago. The company immediately issued a nationwide recall, which cost an immediate $100 million and cut its market share from 37 percent to 7 percent. Then it reintroduced the product with tamper-resistant packaging, offered coupons for free or steeply discounted medicine, and sent out a huge sales force to convince the medical community that the product was now the safest on the market. The result? Public confidence in Tylenol, once nearly destroyed, was almost fully restored.

Managers, like musicians, perform in public—musicians before an audience, managers before their employees, shareholders, and customers. The public nature of the performance creates stress, tempting them to rely on what has worked well in the past. If you play it safe, the rewards tend to be low. But if you lay it all on the line, risking failure, you might just reap huge rewards. "It takes daring to go up in front of 20,000 people and not know what you're going to play," Hart said, adding that usually "[I] tried *not* to think about it, but to instead be open, move with the feeling of that night, maybe fall under a spell and spin a web. That's the fun for me, 'cause I could memorize a solo, or play so fast and so *bad* it would rock your socks off. But I refuse to do it." He continued: "We're always looking for something else, something that you don't find in rigid structures."

That, ultimately, is the lesson for businesses: Rigid

structures, old habits, and excessive caution ultimately lead to failure. What every organization needs is flexibility, the ability to accept the chaos that is the normal state of the world and to keep executing.

They need to improvise—strategically.

2

Live Your Values

How the Dead Did Well
by Doing Good

The message of corporate social responsibility is increasingly important to consumers, and companies are responding. The Body Shop, for example, rejected animal testing long before that practice became widely controversial, began using only nontoxic products, and created a well-funded foundation dedicated to human rights. Interface Carpets committed itself to having zero negative environmental impact. Outdoor gear maker Patagonia helped create 1% for the Planet, a group of businesses committed to donating at least 1 percent of their total sales to protecting the environment. Ice-cream maker Ben & Jerry's—which scored a big hit, and big royalties for Jerry Garcia, with its Cherry Garcia flavor—strives to demonstrate "a deep respect for human beings inside and outside our company and for the communities in which they live." The founder of TOMS Shoes noticed that kids in many developing countries suffer from soil-borne parasites because they don't have shoes. In response, the company started its "One for One" program, in which for every pair of shoes purchased, another pair is donated to a child in need.

Terms such as "corporate social responsibility" weren't on the radar in the 1960s and '70s, when the Grateful Dead became a business phenomenon. For the Dead, treating people and the planet well had nothing to do with eco-chic or brand differentiation. Instead, the Dead became one of the first socially conscious businesses because they embraced deeply held values—kindness, compassion, respect for others—rooted in the sixties counterculture but timeless in their wisdom. It was loyalty to those values that kept the band together for three decades, through upheaval and tragedy. Devotion to principle meant that the band was about more than the music, more than the products they were selling. Deadheads remained loyal to the band because of not only the music but also the ideals they shared. Values build loyalty, and loyalty leads to longevity and bigger long-term profits. Companies should embrace a broader sense of values, in other words, not only because it's the right thing to do but because it's the profitable thing to do.

In the seminal book *In Search of Excellence*, Tom Peters and Robert Waterman emphasized that strong values, broadly conceived, are a hallmark of the best companies. Such companies function more efficiently because "people way down the line know what they are supposed to do in most situations because the handful of guiding values is crystal clear." As a result, "companies whose only articulated goals were financial did not do nearly as well financially as companies that had broader sets of values." By focusing on ideals rather than on money, companies end up making more money. This is a lesson that the Dead learned long ago.

> **Grateful Dead Business Lesson 2:** Embrace strong corporate values and socially conscious business practices because it's the right thing to do—and because it's more profitable.

How the Dead Built a Values Culture

There are many ways to create a corporate culture. Anyone who's spent a little time in the business world has likely suffered through exercises meant to build teamwork and instill corporate values. You know the drill: ropes courses, trust falls, scavenger hunts, and relay races. Or perhaps your company has conducted a "360-degree assessment," so managers can get candid feedback from peers, colleagues, and superiors and better understand how deeply the company's values are felt. Such measures can be useful, but the problem is that they tend to be one-shot deals that can't possibly reach deeply enough to affect a company's real culture. The Dead, on the other hand, forged one of the strongest organizational cultures imaginable, without relying on gimmicky one-off training. Instead, they lived through the sixties together. Everyone in the organization understood and embraced the values of this cultural revolution, and their common devotion to that era's principles ensured their long-term success and profitability.

The Grateful Dead formed just as the Bay Area was emerging as the epicenter of the sixties counterculture. The movement was galvanized by support for civil rights and opposition to the Vietnam War, but its challenge to American society was more fundamental than any one issue. The counterculture sought to reject all received wisdom, all authority, and all assumptions, and to build a new type of society on the basis of peace, love, harmony, and trust. It was a revolutionary movement, and the Dead were at its center, absorbing its wisdom and contributing to the cause. Central to the Dead's organizational values was a belief in community, which would shape the band's extraordinary generosity toward its employees, its fans, and society at large. Surprisingly, this sense of community was forged in part through the experience of psychedelic drugs. Jerry Garcia recalled that his first acid trip, in 1965, changed his life, confirming that life was "a series of continually opening doors." LSD, legal in California until 1966, often gave users a feeling that the universe was stitched together in inexplicable but profound ways, that boundaries—between life and death, the dream state and waking, one person and another—were illusory rather than real. This realization had crucial implications for the Dead's business practices. Unlike most bands—and most businesses—which saw strict divisions between producer and consumer, musicians and fans, the Dead always believed they were united with the Deadheads in the common enterprise of making music and making the world a better place. This commitment to community built extraordinarily close relationships both within the organization and between the band and its fans. The band's path of building community by taking drugs cannot, of course, be followed by businesses today. But by examining how the Dead created their culture, any organization can better understand how to chart its own course toward bedrock values and business success.

First, they put their sense of community to the test by living together. In the fall of 1966 the band members moved into an old Victorian house at 710 Ashbury Street in San Francisco. Lesh and Kreutzmann and their girlfriends kept an apartment nearby, but the two couples spent most of their days with the rest of the band at 710. Residents included Garcia, Ron "Pigpen" McKernan (the band's original keyboardist, who died in 1973), and Weir; manager Rock Scully and his girlfriend Tangerine;

Danny Rifkin and two equipment men, Laird Grant and Bob Matthews. Carolyn "Mountain Girl" Adams, who had recently borne a child fathered by Ken Kesey, became Garcia's girlfriend (and, later, his wife), and the two settled into a domestic routine.

As 710 became the family home of the Dead, it also became the nerve center for Haight-Ashbury. The door of 710 was never locked, not even at night, and all of hippie San Francisco wandered into the house to talk or share a joint or scrounge for food. Richard Goldstein, a rock critic for the *Village Voice*, spent some time at 710. As a hard-bitten New Yorker, he was suspicious of the Dead and the whole sixties vibe, but he came away convinced. "It worked," he said. "All the hierarchies of status that applied in New York weren't there, and the way the Dead lived was sort of the essence of this notion, and that's what I regarded as so heroic." Many others saw the same thing. "Our place got to be a center of energy and people were in there organizing stuff," Garcia recalled. "There would be a lot of motion, a lot of energy exchanged, and it was all real high in those days because at the time the Haight-Ashbury was a community.... It was just a very small neighborhood affair [and] we were all working for each other's benefit." Here lay the foundations of the Dead's values: a close group of people living together, working together, and welcoming the larger community to share their experiences with them.

The band built this idea of community into their

performing lives. Ken Kesey, who had become famous after publishing *One Flew Over the Cuckoo's Nest* in 1962, began hosting events known as Acid Tests. These "happenings" featured bizarre costumes, colored lights, strange performances, experimental films, and music by the Grateful Dead. Crucially, the Acid Tests were communal undertakings, with no paid performers and a shared responsibility by everyone present to create the entertainment. Similar in spirit was the "Human Be-In," held in San Francisco's Golden Gate Park in January 1967. You can't understand the Grateful Dead—their music, their fans, their long career—without grasping the spirit of the Human Be-In. The event, billed as "A Gathering of the Tribes," was intended to bring together the various aspects of the youth scene: Beat poets, Berkeley political radicals, rock 'n' roll bands, hippies. Timothy Leary, the Harvard psychologist turned LSD evangelist, put a flower behind each ear and intoned his famous slogan, "Turn on, tune in, drop out." Owsley "Bear" Stanley, Grateful Dead soundman and the Bay Area's top LSD producer, passed out samples from his latest batch. Jerry Rubin contributed an antiwar speech, and Gary Snyder, Lawrence Ferlinghetti, and Allen Ginsberg read poems. Quicksilver Messenger Service, Jefferson Airplane, and the Grateful Dead played sets.

But the speakers, bands, and prayers were only part of the event. Just as important were the people in the crowd, who played flutes and drums, tossed Frisbees, wandered through the trees, and flew kites. When children became lost, the Hell's Angels—yes, the Hell's Angels—helped reunite them with their parents. Even the cops got into the spirit, staying on the fringes so they wouldn't have to address the fact that so many people were smoking marijuana. At the end of the day, Ginsberg said it would be nice to leave the park clean. The crowd set to work, gathering up sandwich wrappers, wine bottles, and paper, so that not a speck of trash remained. "It was another miracle," one participant reported, "and in some ways this was more disturbing to the square community than a ton of refuse would have been." The *San Francisco Chronicle* music critic Ralph Gleason summed up the event for the next day's paper: "No fights. No drunks. No troubles. Two policemen on horseback and 20,000 people.... Saturday's gathering was an affirmation, not a protest. A statement of life, not death, and a promise of good, not evil." That was the organizational promise the Dead embraced, and kept, in 1967 and for the rest of their careers. Life, not death. Good, not evil. Those were the defining values of the era and the bedrock business values on which the Dead built their success.

Obviously companies today can't re-create the experience of participating in an emergent counterculture. Every company must find its own way to build a values system and to create a business that is bigger, and more meaningful, than the products and services it offers. The Dead happened to find their path in 1960s San

Francisco, and they followed it to business success for the next thirty years. As we'll see throughout this book, devotion to kindness, trust, and harmony led the band to reward their employees with high salaries, generous benefits, and a share in decision making; and it led them to devote enormous resources to making sure their fans were treated fairly.

How the Dead Put Their Values to Work

The band's charitable donation of proceeds from *Built to Last* was just one of the ways they put their principles into practice. The Dead's values kept them on course throughout their three-decade career because everyone in the organization was committed to principles more profound than simply making money. And for the Dead, it wasn't enough simply to believe in those values. They not only talked the talk but also walked the walk, by doing charitable work to help the larger community. What's more, the band's good deeds proved inspirational to fans and made them even more committed to the Dead. Given the rising tide of socially conscious consumers, businesses today should take heed of the Dead's model.

It should be said that being socially conscious need not involve becoming entangled in politics. The Dead were very cautious about getting involved in partisan battles, and they turned down all politicians—including the Mondale and Hart presidential campaigns—who tried to buy access to the band's mailing list. Though generally liberal, Garcia distrusted politicians and "every asshole who told people what to do," as he put it. But the Dead did support causes that aligned with their values. They had been inspired, in the late sixties, by the anarchist group the Diggers, who supported a radical anti-corporate, anti-profit stance and idolized the word *free*. They scrounged and stole food to feed the homeless and hippies of San Francisco, and espoused free music and dancing in the streets. The Dead were never that radical, but they took up the spirit of the times by collaborating with the Diggers on free shows. All the band needed was a sunny day, a flatbed truck parked on the street for a stage, and an extension cord run through the window of someone's apartment. The Dead liked to play, and they liked to see people dance—what better way to achieve that than to play for free on the streets? As Weir said, "the point of everything was to make enough money so we could play for free."

They played for free quite a bit, because they wanted to support organizations whose values they shared. Among nonprofit groups looking to raise money, the Dead became known as a soft touch for benefit shows. "Garcia would say yes to almost everyone," manager Rock Scully said. "Somebody died, we'd do a concert. The Zen Buddhists wanted to take over this piece of property? We'd do that. The creamery was failing in Eugene or Spring-field? Let's go fix that." It continued long past the six-ties. In 1988 the band bailed out a save-the-rainforest fund-raiser that was on the verge of collapse. "Some-body needs to do something," Garcia said in his typi-cally self-effacing way. "It's just incredibly pathetic that it has to be us." The benefit, at Madison Square Garden, raised a quarter of a million dollars. A follow-up Grateful Dead tribute album, featuring performances from Elvis Costello, Lyle Lovett, and others, added over $1 million more to the rainforest cause.

Despite the good causes, it was not always sweetness and light. There were too many situations in which free shows contributed to infighting within the recipient organization, and sometimes lawsuits resulted. In a par-ticularly egregious case, a 1982 benefit for Vietnam vet-erans resulted in a battle among organizers that wasted most of the money raised.

The Dead decided to impose more order on their char-itable work. In 1984 they created the Rex Foundation, named after the late crewmember Rex Jackson. Each year they would dedicate a certain run of shows to char-ity, with all proceeds going to the foundation. Though Deadheads likely would have paid more for a good cause, the Dead held ticket prices steady because they wanted the donations to come from the band, not from their fans. All their profits went toward the foundation, and the foundation distributed the money in increments of

$5,000 and $10,000. Garcia later began donating his royalties from Cherry Garcia ice cream to the foundation.

The foundation's board, which included band members and close associates, including Bill Graham and basketball great Bill Walton, made the decisions. Groups could not apply for funds; rather, this "circle of deciders" simply showered money upon deserving groups and individuals, which ranged from avant-garde composers (Lesh's choice); to groups advocating for AIDS patients, the environment, and the homeless; to the 1992 Lithuanian Olympic basketball team (which received tie-dyed warm-up suits as well as money). In characterizing the band's philosophy of giving, Garcia said they primarily supported "low-profile, direct-action kind of stuff. That's the most appealing stuff to deal with because it's easy to see that the money is—that something real is happening, so it doesn't get caught in the overhead scuffle that characterizes a lot of big charity." According to Weir, the motivation for giving was "enlightened self-interest.... In order to make the world we live in a more livable place, we have to work on it a bit." Between 1984 and 1995, the foundation gave away more than $7.4 million.

"Enlightened self-interest" is a good way to describe all of the Dead's business dealings. Charitable activities, performed out of selflessness, became an important part of the Dead's brand. Deadheads liked being associated with a band that supported good causes, and that spirit has carried on down to the present. When the Grateful Dead stopped touring in 1995, the Rex Foundation lost its main source of funding and, for a time, gave out relatively few donations. Then, after 2000, the group was revitalized by surviving band members, employees, and fans who didn't want the Dead's charitable vision to wane. Because it could no longer rely exclusively on the band's financial support, the foundation began to solicit donations from fans and others who believed in the mission. There's even a Facebook group called South Florida Fans of the Rex Foundation, which spreads the word about Dead-related events and encourages donations. The foundation, once an expression of the Dead's values, became an expression of Deadhead values as well. This is the sort of undertaking that convinces fans they're doing more than listening to music—they're participating in something with meaning. That's why fans have stuck with the band for what is now four and a half decades—buying records and merchandise, and giving to a charity founded by the Dead. By helping the world, the Dead have helped themselves. By doing good, they've done well. Of the band's values-driven approach, Weir said, "All I can suggest is that people give it a try. It's worked real well for us."

Let Values Drive Your Business

People for whom values are important expect their work environment to respect those values. This was certainly true of the Grateful Dead, and it paid off. The band underwent tremendous stresses over three decades of playing, and their devotion to higher principles held them together. "If [employees] have a strong base of unchanging bedrock values, they are better equipped to weather any storm," Tom Morris wrote in *If Aristotle Ran General Motors.* "When both employer and employee know that they share a foundation of basic values, such as the four transcendent values of truth, beauty, goodness and unity, along with the aligned values of respect, integrity, trustworthiness, then they can move forward together with some measure of confidence despite tremendous change." Those transcendent principles formed the bedrock of success for the Dead—and could do the same for any business.

The Cone Cause Evolution 2007 survey found that 87 percent of Americans would switch brands if the new company were associated with a good cause—up from 66 percent in 1993. The trend toward supporting socially conscious brands is strongest among the young. So-called Generation Y, people currently in their twenties, overwhelmingly describe themselves as committed to making the world a better place. According to a survey in *Business Week*, 61 percent of this generation feels personally responsible for making a difference in the world; 69 percent consider a company's social commitment when deciding where to shop; and 89 percent are likely to switch brands to support a cause. The next generation of workers and consumers, in other words, has become committed to "ethical consumerism," the notion that businesses, and the customers who support them, can play a major role in the fostering of environmental health and human rights. When it came to values-driven business, the Dead were way ahead of the game. Now the rest of the world is catching up, and businesses who wish to find employees and customers within this demographic might be wise to follow the example of the Dead.

The Dead's values animated everything they did in business. In fact, their focus on living their values was one reason they struggled as a business for so long: trying too hard to make a buck seemed a pathetic goal when their real hope was to change the world. But it was a commitment that eventually paid off. The Dead embraced life, not death; community, not isolation; freedom, not restriction; harmony, not conflict. It was their integrity, and their commitment to the greater good, that won them the intense loyalty of their fans and their long success in the music business.

"We would all like to be able to live an uncluttered life, a simple life, a good life," Garcia said, "and think about moving the whole human race ahead a step or a few steps." Those are worthy goals for any business to pursue.

3

Be Kind to Your Customers

How the Dead Offered Superior Customer Value

Customer service is both an old and a relatively new concept. It's old in the sense that, for most of our history, people did their shopping at local stores where loyalty was built on personal relationships. That situation changed only in the years after World War II, when retailing went regional and national, with a corresponding loss of personal connection. In addition, manufacturing in America—the only major economy to survive the war intact—grew powerful but also sluggish and sloppy due to a lack of competition. Japan, when it was rebuilding from the war, decided to be second to none in manufacturing. Japanese companies hired experts, including the American consultant William Edwards Deming, who taught the importance of statistical quality control and "zero-defect" manufacturing—resulting in products and services that made customers very happy. By the 1980s, Ford recognized its own problems with quality control and customer satisfaction. It recruited Deming to institute what became known as Total Quality Management, or TQM, a management program dedicated to creating high-quality products, serving customers, and ensuring their loyalty.

The business world's intense focus on customer service, then, dates only as far back as the 1980s. Today the companies most celebrated for fulfilling this legacy include Southwest Airlines, Lexus, and Zappos, which display deep respect for their customers by offering the highest quality products and services. The Dead, though, were way ahead of the game. They insisted on the highest quality practices for manufacturing records, the best sound systems, and the most attentive customer service in their mail-order business. Jerry Garcia once articulated a key difference between the Grateful Dead and the Rolling Stones. "Their attitude is different," Garcia said. "There's antagonism there. It's one of the classic rock 'n' roll attitudes, it's the punk attitude. I dig it, but it's not what we do. We're friendly. For me, I can't see relating to the audience any other way. We exist by their grace. It's very hard for me to do anything but like them. They're nice people." The Dead were nice people; their fans were nice people. The simple principle of kindness was central to the Dead. In "Uncle John's Band," Garcia asks a question that sums up the Dead worldview: "What I want to know is, are you kind?"

The band's dedication to customer service grew from their ethical code: they were committed to treating people well simply because that was the right thing to do. The band was kind to the fans. And the fans were kind to the band. Be kind: it may seem like a *Sesame Street* sort of lesson, but it actually requires a radical commitment, placing substantial demands on a company and sacrifices in short-term profitability. In the end, though, it pays off.

Grateful Dead Business Lesson 3: Be kind to your customers—by offering high-quality products and services and being responsive to their concerns—and they'll be kind to you by becoming lifelong customers.

Sell Only the Best

Despite the Dead's popular image as zonked-out hippies, they were deeply committed to providing a high-quality experience for their fans. As early as 1967, when the band was playing shows in San Francisco, Garcia would tell his bandmates, "This isn't an Acid Test anymore, boys and girls. They're paying money to come and see us. We have to put on a show." The Acid Tests had been

"happenings," where the Dead were just fellow partici-
pants, and could play as much or as little as they wanted.
But now they had paying customers. Garcia "was very
professional about it," Rock Scully recalled. "Jerry was
the guy who instructed the band that we were now
getting into show business and the people were paying money to come and see us, so we had to be good."
During a tour in 1968, Lesh was feeling uncharacteristi-
cally uncomfortable onstage, as if the music were reach-
ing beyond what he was capable of. At one point, he
just stopped playing, bewildered. Between sets, Garcia
confronted him. "He was so pissed, he just grabbed me
and said, 'You play, motherfucker,' and sort of threw me
down the stairs." They were in show business now, and
show business demanded that musicians actually put on
a show.

While demanding stellar showmanship of themselves,
the Dead stayed committed to keeping ticket prices at a
reasonable level. "We have always tried to keep our ticket
prices down mainly because we cannot imagine why anyone would want to pay eight dollars to watch somebody
play music," Weir said in the early seventies. "That is
just a lot of money." The Dead even took care of those
who couldn't afford tickets at all. For their fall 1971 East
Coast tour, they arranged FM broadcasts to satisfy fans
without tickets. By the late 1980s and early 1990s, when
the band's popularity forced them to play more stadium
shows, they found new ways to be kind to fans and offer

value. "The band in general, and Jerry in particular, were always very conscious of giving the kids their money's worth," according to John Scher, a band employee during that period. "That's why they put huge opening acts on the bill with them—Bob Dylan; Tom Petty; Crosby, Stills and Nash; Sting; Traffic; Steve Miller." Even with these high-earning, heavyweight second acts, ticket prices remained low. If other bands' stadium shows were thirty dollars a ticket, the Dead set theirs at twenty-five dollars. For the same reason, the Dead were quick to adopt oversize video screens for their stadium shows. It was "a matter of conscience," Garcia said, to make sure everyone could not only hear great sound but see the band as well.

These may seem like obvious choices, but many bands took a different path, charging exorbitant prices for tickets and making do with cheaper, less talented opening acts. The Dead, though, sacrificed short-term profitability in order to treat their fans well, and they ended up forming valuable customer relationships that ensured long-term profit. "They had an ethic about the person in the backseat, the far back," staffer Alan Trist once said while discussing the band's enormous investment in sound systems. Because the person in back had paid the same ticket price as the person in the front row, both deserved to hear the same thing—it was only fair. "I think that's indicative of everything they did right there," Trist said.

Listen to Your Customers

On the jacket of the 1971 live album *Grateful Dead*, the band printed a note to its fans:

DEAD FREAKS UNITE
Who are you? Where are you? How are you?
Send us your name and address and we'll keep you informed.

Initially, 350 people responded. But then the letters kept flooding into the office, and the band expanded its efforts to keep in touch with fans. "We'd set up our own booth at concerts and give away postcards and sign people up for our mailing list," said Steve Brown, a record company employee. There were ten thousand names on the mailing list in 1972, twenty-six thousand in 1973, forty thousand in 1974. And the list kept growing, until, by the early eighties, there were ninety thousand names on it.

Most bands would have used such a mailing list to create a traditional fan club: fans would pay an annual fee and, in return, get a slick newsletter and an opportunity to buy glossy photos and other band merchandise. The Dead, though, didn't create a paid fan club. Instead, they wrote a newsletter that was sent out for free. Garcia and Hunter would produce four- and eight-page missives filled with a tour schedule, news about the band, and a bizarre collection of drawings by Garcia, poems, and offbeat philosophizing. The lack of dues or subscription fees meant the band swallowed the costs—about $15,000 to mail out each issue. The Dead didn't want their communications with their fans to be just another revenue stream. They undertook a venture that was riskier and more forward-looking, with the goal of building deeper relationships with their fans. In the late 1970s, for instance, there was a "Deadheads Only" tour of smaller venues, with tickets available only to fans on the mailing list.

Most important was the sense of connection the mailing list offered to fans—the feeling that their views really mattered. The mailing list was more than just a way for the Dead to communicate with the fans. The Dead wanted to make sure their fans were happy. But how could they know for sure? Communication between rock bands and fans tends to be a one-way street, with the band making noise and the fans listening. But the Dead wanted something different—not a hierarchy but a collaboration. So they asked for their fans to talk to them, and the fans were happy to oblige. The go-between for fans and the band was an employee named Eileen Law, who began overseeing the list in 1972 and who became "the spiritual mother of all Dead Heads." Law opened all the mail that fans sent to the band—and that often meant fifty or more letters a day. "I read every letter that comes," Law said. If the letter was addressed to a specific band member, she made sure it got to him.

Fans sent in their original poems and artwork, in the interest of artistic exchange. They wrote long, articulate letters testifying to what the band meant to them. And they expressed concern and kindness: when Garcia was hospitalized with throat problems in the late seventies, he received thousands of get-well cards. Often those writing in to buy tickets received not only tickets but also handwritten notes from the staff.

Eileen Law's mailbox also served as a sort of national suggestion/complaint box for Dead fans. And unlike most similar boxes, this one actually had some effects. *The Grateful Dead Anthology*, a songbook of fifty tunes, was in a sense edited by fans: "The songs we chose to include were the ones most requested by the letters," Trist said. "Eileen kept track, and that's what we did." Complaints, too, prompted action. "Please change your repertoire. It's become rather boring in the last few years hearing the same songs all the time," one fan wrote. So many fans wrote in to complain that they didn't like one particular song—"Keep Your Day Job"—that the Dead dropped it from their repertoire.

Other fans suggested what venues to avoid in particular cities—"the band really pays attention to those," Law said. "Specific complaints about producers or a hall's acoustics or maybe just general comments about the direction of the band, I pass those on, too, and they [the band members] really do listen," Law said. Alan Trist, who assisted with the fan communication, agreed. "It's the feedback, the letters, that makes this work," he said. "We spread them out on a table and use them as the basis for many of the decisions we make—halls, producers—and send relevant complaints to producers." In other words, if particular shows didn't go well—bad acoustics, overly aggressive security, overpriced parking—the fans would let the Dead know, and the Dead would let the venue know, and things would change. Responsiveness like that let Dead fans know that the Dead cared about them, and respected their opinions. This—along with great music, of course—was the foundation of fan loyalty.

The Dead had to work hard to create and maintain this mailing list in a time when communication—by phone and letter—was slow and complicated. These days the Internet and wireless communication make it easier than ever before for businesses to know what their customers are thinking. And customers aren't shy about expressing their feelings, both directly to the companies and through media such as Twitter, Facebook, Yelp, and Amazon reviews. Too many companies, however, don't know what to do with this wealth of information. Customers know that occasionally they'll experience a disappointing product or service, whether it's a faulty cell phone or a concert venue with bad sound. If the business makes it right—by apologizing and replacing the phone, or deciding not to play that venue again—the customer generally will be satisfied, and according to marketing research, perhaps even more committed than ever before. If you respond to that complaint with begrudging customer service, however, you've lost a customer for good.

Customers know mistakes will happen, but they demand to be listened to. The Dead went out of their way to find a way to collect fan feedback in an era when it was difficult. Even better, they put that feedback to work to improve the fan experience.

Sell the Brand

How did the Dead turn that loyalty into profits? Through record sales, concert ticket sales, and, more surprisingly, merchandising. By the 1990s the Dead had built one of the most sophisticated and profitable merchandising operations in the music business. The Dead and merchandise are a natural fit. Buying branded merchandise is a statement of identity and a physical manifestation of loyalty. Deadheads, so thoroughly devoted to their band, were some of the most avid consumers among rock fans. They wanted to show their colors and mark themselves as members of the tribe.

The Dead "started the trend of marketing band paraphernalia," according to Garcia biographer Blair Jackson. Two primary factors helped the Dead achieve this status. First, the Marin County artists Alton Kelley and Stanley "Mouse" Miller had created a number of iconic images—including the skeleton crowned with roses—for the Dead's album covers. Those images functioned as band logos, and they worked beautifully on T-shirts. The second factor in the Dead's merchandising success was the mailing list, that database of names and addresses for the band's most committed fans. As it turned out, the band's newsletter, which had been created to keep the band in touch with fans, also worked for direct marketing. One of the first Dead newsletters advertised band T-shirts for sale through a shop called Kumquat Mae, identified as "the Dead's old ladies' store." That shop was co-owned by Susila Kreutzmann, wife of the Dead drummer; she also sold Dead T-shirts at Bill Graham's concert venue, Winterland Ballroom, in the early 1970s. When Graham noticed how fast the shirts were selling, he took over the operation and turned it into Winterland Products, which pioneered rock merchandising and was a giant in the field for decades. In earlier years, T-shirts weren't a standard part of the rock 'n' roll tour, but Graham's new business signed contracts with the Dead and other bands to design and manufacture tour T-shirts. At each stop on the tour, the band would sell the shirts, with proceeds split among Winterland, the band, and the concert venue. From this simple concept a mighty industry was born.

The Dead rode the wave. Although through the years

the band had deals with industry giants such as Winterland and Brockum Merchandising, in the early 1990s
they decided to "insource" merchandising. As with the
decisions on record company and ticket sales, the move
was motivated by a desire to serve customers better and
to produce more revenue. And it worked beautifully.
Peter McQuaid, who earlier had helped found a company
to manage fan clubs for rock bands, became director of
Grateful Dead Merchandising. Before long, merchandise
sales at concerts had doubled to an average of two dollars
per concertgoer.

Then the Dead looked beyond simply selling at concerts, transforming themselves into the "rock world's
answer to L.L.Bean." The old newsletters were replaced
by *The Grateful Dead Almanac*—part fan magazine,
part catalog. The *Almanac* was sent out quarterly to
140,000 people, about half of whom could be considered active customers, who chose from among hundreds
of items, including golf balls and baby clothes embla-
zoned with Dead logos. In the three years leading up to
Garcia's death and the band's demise, sales of non-music
merchandise rose at a rate of 25 percent a year. In 1994,
the band's last full year of touring, the Dead earned $35
million in sales from non-music merchandise. That figure rose to $45 million in 1995. Sales remained strong
after the band broke up: in the late 1990s, Grateful
Dead Productions was shipping a thousand packages a
day. Even today at Dead.net, the band's official Web site,

you can buy a multitude of items, including Mother of Pearl Bolt Earrings, a Steal Your Face Messenger Bag, Dancing Skeleton Flip Flops, a Dancing Bear Wrist Sweatband, Warlocks Full Zip Jacket, and Jerry Garcia Silk Neckties.

A few old fans might have griped about the commercialization, but many more saw the merchandise—and treasured it—for what it was: a direct link between the band and its fans, a way for fans to express their devotion to the music that meant so much to them. The Dead weren't so much exploiting their image as using it to do what they did best: fostering a sense of community. Along the way, they also made millions of dollars.

The Virtuous Cycle

After Jerry Garcia's death in 1995, many Deadheads expressed their emotions in part by buying gear, and the mail-order business worked around the clock to fulfill orders. In the week after Garcia's August death, order calls came in at a rate of fifteen thousand a day. The first copy of the catalog after the tragedy included a note to fans: "Deadheads have expressed an overwhelming desire to have something...anything...some music, a memento, an amulet, a power object...to console them, to inspire them, to remind them of the good times. And it's our privilege to be able to provide these things."

The Dead produced good live shows and were responsive to fans, which generated fan loyalty. Loyal fans, in turn, wanted to fly the flag by wearing Grateful Dead gear. They bought this gear from Grateful Dead Merchandising, which, like the band itself, offered high-quality products, fair prices, and stellar customer service and responsiveness. The result, of course, was increased fan loyalty. You might call this the "virtuous cycle" of good customer service. In *The Loyalty Effect*, Frederick Reichheld pointed out that the average company loses half of its customers every five years. "Inventories of experienced customers" are a company's "most valuable asset," Reichheld said. "You cannot *control* a human inventory, which of course has a mind of its own, so you must *earn* its loyalty." That the Dead did—in spades.

The business writer Glenn Rifkin has pegged the Dead as pioneers in nontraditional marketing, comparing the band to IAMS pet foods or Snap-on tools, which focused first on creating high-quality products and only later worked out how to turn those products into profits. The Dead pioneered database marketing, focused on going deep with committed fans rather than going broad by appealing to a mass audience. They built an enormous list of fan names and addresses, a project that, in the years before the rise of the personal computer, was not an easy—or an inexpensive—task. They used this database to market to a targeted group of customers, those who had already expressed an interest in the band.

The Dead were not the Beatles; they were too weird for mass appeal. So rather than marketing broadly, they used their database to tie into the passionate support of their most devoted fans. What's more, the Dead offered a simple value proposition: high-quality music at a reasonable price. And they maintained the quality and variety of their performances over decades, giving fans a reason to come back for more. And those dedicated customers were the band's best marketers. Management guru Tom Peters has referred to customers as "appreciating assets," meaning that happy customers share the joy and attract new customers.

"We did it for the people in the audience," roadie Steve Parish explained. "We cared about that music and we put our whole heart and soul into making it as good as we could…" This commitment to stellar customer service resulted in huge profits, and it all stemmed from the Dead's simple ethic of treating their fans with respect. Any business that starts with those principles is already a step ahead. So: Are you kind?

4

Share Your Content

How the Dead Exploited the Power of "Free"

Copyright laws exist, the theory goes, because artists will have more incentive to create if they are given exclusive rights to profit from their work. Trademarks—words, designs, and symbols identifying the producer of a product—are thought to serve as indicators of quality and accountability. Most businesses, including musical acts, enforce their copyrights and trademarks vigorously through the courts.

The Grateful Dead—committed as they were to antiauthoritarian values and a benevolent view of humanity—decided to take a softer approach to these issues. They became famous for allowing fans to record their live shows and to share those tapes with one another. Similarly, for years the band looked the other way as Deadheads created and sold merchandise bearing the band's name and logos. Though they did take legal action against large-scale bootleggers and counterfeiters, they took a gentler approach toward smaller-scale infringement—allowing noncommercial recordings of their music as well as free use of their trademarks by small-scale merchandisers. The music industry had always assumed that allowing people free access to live recordings would cut demand for commercial recordings, damaging the band's income. But a funny thing happened with the Grateful Dead: rather than hurting the band's business, the taping helped. Fans shared the tapes, which drew more fans into the scene. Similarly, small-scale trademark infringement at shows encouraged creativity among fans, and helped build the brand. In these ways the Dead radically upended traditional models of the music business.

In the last two decades, many bands have turned to a revenue stream that looks very much like the Grateful Dead's. In fact, this has become a more general business model for the Internet age. In this new wired world, "pretty much everything is given away for free in some version with the hopes of selling something else," according to Chris Anderson in his recent bestselling book *Free: The Future of a Radical Price*. Not surprisingly, one of the pioneers of this way of thinking was one of the Dead's own, lyricist John Perry Barlow, who cofounded the Electronic Frontier Foundation and penned a seminal article for *Wired* in 1994. "The best way to raise demand for your product is to give it away," Barlow wrote, citing the example of the Dead's taping policy. "The Grateful Dead has increased its popularity enormously by giving [music] away."

An earlier era regarded songs and logos as property to be jealously guarded behind legal barriers; their scarcity, and the bands' ability to sell them, is what brought income. The Dead, by contrast, intuitively understood that their success was linked not to scarcity but to familiarity and accessibility. In this way the Dead, though unaware of it, virtually invented viral marketing. The people who riffed on their logos and traded their tapes became partners of the band, co-marketers who spread the word about the joys of being a Deadhead.

> **Grateful Dead Business Lesson 4:** In creative businesses, familiarity—rather than scarcity—creates value. Share your intellectual property, because the more people who know about your work, the more ways there will be to make money.

Draw Distinctions

The concept of "free," of course, didn't emerge fully formed from the brilliant business minds of the Grateful

Dead. It came about more or less by accident, but the band members were smart enough to grab hold of the idea and profit from it.

In the parking lots outside shows was an area that came to be known as Shakedown Street, after a Dead song of the same name. Starting in the early 1970s, a few fans had started selling hand-designed T-shirts at shows, and this gradually expanded into a much broader scene. The serious vendors would arrive as soon as the lots opened and park in rows, setting up a blue tarp or a booth behind each vehicle. There they sold food (grilled cheese and veggie burritos were standard), jewelry, clothes (especially T-shirts and primitive-print skirts), and alcohol and drugs (primarily beer, marijuana, psychedelics, and nitrous oxide). The best customers were local fans who wanted a memento of the band on the only night of the year they'd see them. The vendors, for the most part, were "tourheads," and they weren't looking to get rich. As one vendor explained, he sold at shows "so we could have food and go to more shows." They wanted to get to the next show because they wanted to experience the warm community of the Grateful Dead, what one writer has called the "communitarian, craftsperson-inspired vision of life on tour."

Among their other wares, the vendors sold items bearing Dead logos, in particular the skull-and-lightning-bolt design known as "Steal Your Face." As Garcia biographer Blair Jackson has written, there were "T-shirts, decals, bumper stickers, tattoos, flags; you name it. There were hundreds of variations on the Dead's most familiar iconography—i.e., adapted from Dead album covers and the like—but thousands more that were completely new inventions or different variations on skeletons, roses, etc." There was a wide variety of merchandise, some straightforwardly borrowing from Dead merchandise, others riffing on the Dead's trademarked icons. The Dead allowed this sort of thing in the early years, cracked down for a couple of misguided years in the late eighties, then wised up and permitted the scene again. One official licensee of Dead merchandise wasn't troubled at all by this low-key infringement. "The Dead love it. So do all of us," he said. "They're not hurting anybody; they're not out to make any huge profit on the Dead's name."

Here was an instance in which trademark infringement promoted creativity. "No group had ever inspired so much creative involvement from its fans," Blair Jackson wrote. John Perry Barlow agreed, harshly criticizing the band for the few years when it cracked down on the scene. "The Deadheads had an open-source creative community for imagery and stuff-making that was a great deal more interesting than what we could do in-house," he said.

Alongside these creative Deadheads, however, were high-volume T-shirt makers who were simply exploiting the scene for cash. At first the Dead didn't know quite what to do with such vendors. At a 1984 band meeting, they discussed a T-shirt bootlegger caught with about five thousand shirts. The meeting minutes suggest the range of discussion: Hunter cautioned against busting them; Weir, joking, thought telling the bootlegger the shirts were "ugly" might be enough to make him stop; Garcia wanted to make sure they were evenhanded with the policy; and Hal Kant, the lawyer, reminded them that in order to maintain their copyrights and trademarks, the band needed to take reasonable steps to enforce them. Clearly, the band's default live-and-let-live values were clashing with the realities of copyright law and the need to keep making money to cover the band's high overhead.

This new class of bootleggers had no relation to the tourheads. They were sophisticated operators who exploited whichever band was hot at the time, bought cheap T-shirts from overseas, had them silkscreened at a half dozen or so major printers, then shipped them to distributors around the country. The distributors then followed the band from show to show, parking a mile or so from the venues and consigning the shirts to peddlers. They dealt in cash, avoiding taxes and licensing fees. They also didn't have to give a cut to the venue. As a result, their prices were much lower than the official tour T-shirts, and they still realized enormous profits—likely 40 percent or more of the retail price. Artists such as the Dead, meanwhile, earned only 10 or 20 percent of the retail price. And for every bootleg shirt sold on the sidewalk, there was one fewer official shirt sold inside. Estimates of the money involved are difficult to make, but it was easily in the tens of millions of dollars.

With these serious bootleggers, the Dead and their licensees played hardball, as court records show. In the late 1970s, for instance, the East Coast chain T-Shirt Barn was selling unlicensed Grateful Dead apparel— until they were slapped with a preliminary restraining order. A year or so later, Dead licensee Winterland Concessions sued a company called Creative Screen Design, which was found to have sold nearly two hundred thousand counterfeit T-shirts bearing the logos of the Dead and other bands. The court ruled that Winterland lost profits totaling $275,204, and the defendants ended up paying Winterland nearly $1 million.

The Dead tolerated, even encouraged, the small-scale T-shirt sellers and sued the large-scale bootleggers. But what about the ones in the middle? Business writer Glenn Rifkin tells the story of Greg Burbank, a young college dropout who was selling high-quality counterfeit T-shirts in a show parking lot one night in the mid-1980s when he was approached by band staff with an offer that surprised him. "Rather than suing us for trademark infringement, they brought us on board," Burbank recalls. He became a licensed maker of Dead merchandise, and eventually sold millions of dollars' worth to retail stores. "These people had a real respect for the band and the music," according to Peter·McQuaid, of

Grateful Dead Merchandising. "It was far more satisfying to have a relationship with someone with high regard for the group."

In the band's response to counterfeiting one can see more evidence of their unusual, flexible, and subtle approach to business. They did not give up and allow everyone to steal their trademarks. Yet they did not play hardball, slapping lawsuits on everyone who ever sold a dancing bear T-shirt. Instead, they sought a middle ground, suing the biggest bootleggers; inviting some makers of high-quality bootlegs to go legit by becoming licensed manufacturers; and letting the small-scale merchandisers make the wildly creative products that gave so much life to the Deadhead scene. It might be argued, in fact, that the creativity of these trademark-infringing Deadheads set the stage for the later success of Grateful Dead Merchandising: they helped build a market and an appetite for Grateful Dead gear, and the band later reaped the rewards. "Free" had set the stage for profits.

Go with the Flow

The same model—giving something away and reaping profits in other ways—worked with regard to the taping of live shows. But it didn't develop as a conscious viral marketing strategy. Instead, a practice allowed for certain reasons (a desire to honor tradition and respect fans)

became a valuable business tool. As strategic improvisers, the Dead retrospectively made sense of their taping
policy and turned it into a brilliant business decision.

Grateful Dead fans did not invent the taping of live
music. Key members of the band and crew, in fact, had
been tapers earlier in their lives. In the early 1960s, when
Garcia traveled to the South and Midwest to hear bluegrass, he brought a tape recorder so he could preserve
the performances he heard. "I loved having the tapes
afterwards and being able to trade them around," Garcia
said. "I think that's healthy stuff." Some jazz fans also
got into taping. "I became sympathetic with the tapers
from when I *was* that person," said Dead soundman Dan
Healy, who before he signed on with the Dead had spent
a lot of time recording jazz in nightclubs.

Taping live shows, then, was not so much a radical
innovation as a holdover, a relic of the fifties and sixties
that the Dead preserved into the far more commercial
world of the seventies and eighties—and an indication
that some of the most forward-looking business ideas
have their roots in the past.

Healy's predecessor as soundman, Owsley "Bear"
Stanley, had been one of the first to realize that, due to
the band's improvising, every show should be caught
on tape. He used seven-inch reels to record their early
shows, including the legendary run at the Fillmore on
February 13–14, 1970. A crewmember dubbed the tapes,
and a copy made its way into the growing tape culture,

where it became much prized and traded widely. Soon ordinary fans realized they didn't need to wait for leaked soundboard tapes; they could make their own. At first they sneaked cheap cassette recorders into auditoriums and made mono tapes with low quality; later they moved on to ever more sophisticated equipment.

Taping, for most of the 1970s, existed in a gray area for the Dead. It was officially unsanctioned, so the tapers typically could not practice their craft openly. In 1980, Blair Jackson, Garcia biographer and longtime Dead-head, referred to tapers as "a neurotic and paranoid lot" due to the stresses of smuggling their tape decks into shows. They hid decks in wheelchairs, tossed them over fences to friends inside, bribed security men, or bought pricey decks small enough to fit in a pocket. One famed taper, Barry Glassberg, attended 352 shows and made 310 tapes. His total would have been higher, but he was caught 20 times and prevented from recording. His preferred method of avoiding detection? Wearing a suit, carrying a briefcase, and putting his deck inside a hollowed-out medical journal. Stadium security would try to weed out tapers at stadium entrances, and some members of the Dead's crew would take the initiative and sweep the crowds to confiscate tape decks.

Although taping in this era was still officially unsanctioned, most often it was tolerated. The band members didn't much care. "If people like it they can certainly keep doing it," Garcia said in 1975. "My responsibility to the notes is over after I've played them. At that point I don't care where they go." Or, as Garcia put it another time, taping was "OK with me, as long as the people who are doing the taping aren't obnoxious about it. . . . I don't want to be authoritarian about it."

In 1976, there were a handful of tapers at each show, but the numbers grew steadily, eventually causing problems. Some tapers began to regard themselves as a privileged lot who should have their choice of spots for taping. According to Healy, "the typical example would be a fourteen-year-old kid and his girlfriend would come to the booth in tears saying, 'Me and my girlfriend stood in line for three hours in the snow to get tickets and when we got to our seats these guys just threw us out saying that they needed that seat to tape.'" Some tapers were guilty of, as Healy put it, "the very things that are most anti–Grateful Dead, which is violating other people's space, general rudeness, and lack of consideration for fellow humans."

At a meeting in 1984 the band considered banning taping altogether. The meeting minutes read, "Do we want to stop taping? Do we want to enforce the clause in our contract rider [forbidding taping]?" Also discussed at this meeting was the creation of a special section for tapers, a step that would be taken "not so much for the tapers, but for the others in the audience." And that is what they did. The band began selling, via mail order, special tickets to a dedicated tapers' section, located just behind the sound booth. There was a clear set of rules: Taping was allowed only in the dedicated section, which required a special ticket, and reel-to-reel decks and video cameras were prohibited. Those who violated these rules were subject to ejection from the venue and confiscation of their equipment. And the band specified that the tapes were for noncommercial use only.

It's important to keep in mind why this step was originally taken: to ease conflict and promote civility among the fans. Nobody at the time considered it a brilliant marketing move. But that's exactly what it turned out to be. Here's how:

- Taping created a historical record of Dead shows. The Dead's music changed for each show, and without the tapers, some of those variations would have been lost to history. Tapers might be considered the Dead's first important archivists, and they fed the obsession that characterizes Deadheads.

- Taping drew in new fans. Because the band's official studio recordings were often less than stellar, these tapes of live shows helped convince new fans of just how good the band could be. It made it cheap to become a fan: for the price of a blank tape, a person could acquire a brilliant Dead performance, and many became lifelong fans. Lesh, for one, thinks this process started helping the band even in the early 1970s.

"Tapes of our shows were now being traded widely around the college circuit," he said, referring to the band's tolerance of tapers as "the best decision we never made."

- By helping create new fans, tapes helped the Dead make money. Many of those who discovered the Dead through shared tapes went on to become fans who bought tickets, records, and merchandise. As Healy put it, taping "creates enthusiasm and it creates fraternity and that in the end sells more records."

- It created a community. In the pre-Internet era, Deadheads traded tapes by mail, using ads in the fan magazines *Dead Relix*, *Golden Road*, *Dupree's Diamond News*, and *Unbroken Chain* to communicate with one another. Fans would trade copies of shows they had for those they didn't. For those who had nothing to share, they could get a copy by sending a blank tape and return postage. And, of course, tapes could always be acquired for trade in the parking lot outside Dead shows. Many fans ended up owning hundreds or thousands of tapes, and debates about the best shows and the best recordings are a central Deadhead bonding ritual. John Perry Barlow described taping as "probably the single most important reason that we have the popularity that we have," because the sharing of tapes formed "the basis of a culture and something weirdly like a religion....A lot of what we are selling is community. That is our main product—it's not music."

The legitimate tapers, who traded but never profited, took part in the larger ethic of the Deadhead community, which revolved around not-for-profit sharing. Deadheads could be harsh with those who violated the ethic by selling tapes or scalping tickets. Policing the group's rules in this way only enforced the cohesiveness of Deadheads. They were a self-regulating community, operating according to a shared ethical code. This type of thing is what turned Deadheads into a group apart, loyal to one another and to the band—and eager to share tapes and spread the word about the Dead.

Virtually all of these benefits can be described in terms of what's now known as viral marketing. The classic example is Hotmail, which appended a line—"Get your private, free e-mail at http://www.hotmail.com"—to every message sent by a user. Recipients read that pitch, signed up for Hotmail, and in turn spread the advertisement further each time they sent an e-mail. Viral marketing generally involves a free product or service and relies on preexisting networks of people to spread the word, creating exponential growth in visibility. Thus Hotmail followed the model the Dead created through its taping policies. The Dead's music could be recorded for free, shared among networks of Dead fans, and passed along to potential new fans as well. The concept of viral marketing was named and described in the 1990s, but the Dead got there first.

The Power of the Familiar

The Dead did not share their songs and logos out of some philosophical position that music should be free. Garcia, at least, clearly had contempt for the view that music belonged to the people and should be free. "Fuck 'people's music,'" he said in a 1974 interview, referring to the concept, as he explained it, "that music belongs to the people and musicians rip them off. That kind of thing really irks me." To get good at music, he explained, you have to work and sacrifice. "For someone to deny the fact that you spent a certain amount of your life working on some sort of discipline and learning how to play…that's the rip-off." And here's the kicker from Garcia: "Anytime someone comes down on artists and claims their work on any level, I think that's pure bullshit. There's been too many great musicians who died poor."

The Dead insisted that playing music was labor deserving of pay. As to *how* they got paid—well, that was open to negotiation. And that's what made them truly radical business innovators. They didn't want to go around slapping lawsuits on anyone who taped a show or sold a Dead T-shirt. No fans of the American legal system, the band members were more than willing to tweak the rules in ways that better suited their view of the way the world should be. To the law, a fan selling a tie-dyed T-shirt with a hand-drawn Steal Your Face logo had violated a trademark, just as a major bootlegger with ten thousand badly printed T-shirts had. To the law, a taper recording a show at Madison Square Garden was violating copyright, just like a counterfeiter pressing fake copies of *Wake of the Flood*. The Dead, though, had the wisdom to make distinctions—to distinguish tapers and true fans from bootleggers. They created their own rules—rules that much of the business world has now come to adopt.

Those rules, we should note, were not instituted for business reasons. The Dead's attitude toward taping went through a gradual transformation, from half-hearted attempts to stop it, to tacit approval, to official sanction in the form of the tapers' section. Even this last step was undertaken not as a marketing strategy but as a way to protect other fans from the rudeness of some tapers. In a *60 Minutes II* appearance in 2003, the surviving members of the band discussed the taping decision with Charlie Rose. Here's a snippet:

ROSE: Nobody can say, "I had the idea that if we let them in there to tape, we'll create this great audience."

HART: No. No way! That was not...

ROSE: "And in the end they will look back at us as entrepreneurial geniuses."

HART: Not so. It's not so.

ROSE: You lucked out.

WEIR: Yeah.

HART: We lucked out.

ROSE: They were taping, and you let them have it.

HART: The Grateful Dead is all about luck.

Weir and Hart, in fact, were not giving themselves and the rest of the band quite enough credit. It's true they didn't know taping would turn out to be a brilliant business move. But you could say the Dead created this new business model the same way they did everything else— by improvising a solution on the fly, by retrospectively understanding recent events and using this understanding to shape the future. They were led to that model by the same factors that produced much of their success: respect for their fans, willingness to collaborate with their audience, unwillingness to be authoritarian, and recognition of the facts on the ground. The Dead, true to their values, didn't *want* to crack down on taping. Similarly, musicians and other artists today *cannot* control the sharing and distribution of their work, simply because of the nature of digital information. The challenge back then, as now, was to find a way to allow some sharing of content while still preserving ways of making a living. Such a challenge demands a new business model.

"What people today are beginning to realize is what became obvious to us back then—the important correlation is the one between familiarity and value, not scarcity and value," John Perry Barlow said. "Adam Smith taught that the scarcer you make something, the more valuable it becomes. In the physical world, that works beautifully. But we couldn't regulate [taping at] our shows, and you can't online. The Internet doesn't behave that way. But here's the thing: if I give my song away to twenty people, and they give it to twenty people, pretty soon everybody knows me, and my value as a creator is dramatically enhanced. That was the value proposition with the Dead."

5

Create a Business Tribe

How the Dead Collaborated
with the Deadheads

Harley-Davidson has been described as the prototypical "lifestyle brand." The motorcycle company inspires such visceral passion that riders wear the gear, get tattoos of the logo, make pilgrimages to factories, and generally organize their lives around their bikes. Much as the Dead became identified with joy, experimentation, and kindness, the Harley brand became shorthand for freedom, individualism, and rebellion. Other manufacturers designed heavy cruising bikes to mimic the Harley style, but they couldn't re-create "the lifestyle and total experience of a Harley—from the bike itself to the clothes and rallies and cachet," Glenn Rifkin and Sam Hill explain in *Radical Marketing.* Customers turned Harley into something much more than a motorcycle company—it became a community, a culture, a tribe.

In the twenty-first century, social media outlets have made it easier than ever for people to form themselves into affinity groups of passionate customers, devoted to products as varied as Harry Potter movies, *Star Trek,* American Girl dolls, and the iPad. The Internet, however, has given a further twist to the lifestyle brand model. Not only are consumers creating lifestyles around certain products, but they are also breaking down the distinction between producers and consumers and reshaping the very meaning of the brands. Corporate brands have become a negotiation between companies and consumers, with neither in full control. Once upon a time, it was enough for corporations to know their customers, but now the reverse is true: Customers know their corporations and use the power of the Web to influence corporate decisions. When customers create a lifestyle and sense of identity around a product, they are no longer passive consumers—they are stakeholders, and they demand a say in the meaning of the brand. The consulting firm Deloitte LLP has in recent years been conducting an annual survey called "Tribalization of Business," which seeks to understand and leverage the potential of such communities of customers.

Companies who seek to understand this process would

be wise to pay attention to the Dead, which created a tribe of followers long before the Internet existed. "I was watching the New Year's Eve gig and it was clear to me how tribal it felt," John Perry Barlow once said. "Good communities are tribes. They have rituals and myths and those kind of deeper realities that light up everyday reality and give it some substance." The Deadheads created an entire culture, complete with wardrobe, foods, ethics, and rituals, that gave a powerful sense of meaning to people's lives. What's more, starting way back in the sixties, the Dead did precisely what the Internet is encouraging today: They erased the boundaries between producers and consumers. The band and its fans agreed that the true Grateful Dead experience could be found not in studio albums but in live performances. What's the difference between playing in a studio and playing on a stage? The audience. The Dead simply could not produce their best work unless they were playing before their fans. "I've never experienced it without an audience," Garcia said. "It's just some two-way street." The Dead and Deadheads together created a genuinely collaborative environment in which the band and the fans together produced the organization's greatest product— the live concert performance. The Dead offer a model for the Internet age—how to create a tribe of deeply devoted consumers, and how to collaborate with that tribe to produce better products and more income.

Grateful Dead Business Lesson 5: Harness the power of consumer tribes to collaborate with your customers, improve performance, and boost profits.

How the Dead Created a Tribe

The emergence of the Deadheads was, in part, a result of the Dead's extraordinary customer service. The fans knew that their opinions were important, and that their experiences as fans mattered to the band. The Dead also gave their fans a lot of responsibility, trusting that they would make and share tapes but not sell them. The fans recognized their importance, embraced their responsibility, and built a thriving community around the band. Rebecca Adams, a sociologist who has become the world's foremost expert on Deadhead culture, has focused on the sense of community surrounding the band. She took the position, surprising in the 1980s but taken for granted in the Internet age, that a community can share real fellowship and true feelings even when they are dispersed geographically and able to gather only occasionally. Deadheads lived all over the world, coming together only for the ritual of the live show, yet they shared all the trappings of genuine community. Long before Facebook, Deadheads created their own dispersed social network, a tribe of fans united by a love of the band's music and a commitment to its egalitarian values. This community, in turn, formed the foundation of the Dead's business model.

Modern American society had fragmented in the 1960s, destroying people's sense of connection, and the Dead helped fill a void. According to John Perry Barlow, America had been "erasing the whole idea of community, and people need that desperately." First-time attendees at Dead shows were often surprised that so many of the fans seemed to know one another and greet one another warmly. Adams relates that after a run of Dead shows in Greensboro, North Carolina, police officers marveled that "the Deadheads they had arrested had a reunion in the van where they were being held, embracing one another and exchanging news about mutual friends rather than worrying about the situation facing them." In her research, Adams has found that "Deadheads describe their relationships as intense and intimate. Trust, openness, and the sharing of resources are assumed." At each concert, the fans got together again, caught up on old times, and renewed their sense of togetherness. Ten or 15 percent of attendees at each concert had traveled far enough that they needed to spend a night away from home. An average of three hundred or so cars and vans filled with tourheads followed the band from show to show. In the summer, the number of tourheads would peak at around five thousand. After Garcia died and the band split up, many continued to attend concerts by the remaining band members primarily to keep up with their Deadhead friends.

How did this tribal community emerge? Here's what we can learn from the Dead's example:

1. Encourage inclusiveness:

Garcia biographer Blair Jackson objected to "the straight media's portrayal of Deadheads as stoned, tie-dye-wearing, VW-van-driving, stringy-haired, patchouli-scented, weirdly named, monosyllabic crazies." It's true that more than a few Deadheads matched that description, but many more did not. Most, in fact, functioned just fine in mainstream society but simply liked to let their hair down at Dead shows. Other than a shared commitment to the band and its values, Deadheads were a diverse bunch. "There is very little unanimity on any subject in the band, the organization, or the Deadhead community," according to David Gans, host of the syndicated radio show *The Grateful Dead Hour.* David Shenk and Steve Silberman, authors of a Grateful Dead dictionary, said a Deadhead might be "a Radical Faerie or a neurosurgeon," because "sincere appreciation for the music, and sharing it with others, comes before job title, national identity, and political or religious affiliation." By being open and inclusive themselves, the Dead inspired the same spirit in their community of fans—and this allowed the number of Deadheads to grow and grow.

2. Don't micromanage:

Many companies make the mistake of trying to be too controlling. Walmart, for instance, has created both "The Hub," an online community for teens, and a similar community for "Walmart Moms." The first failed, the second is gasping for air. The problem is that Walmart focused too much on corporate messaging and too little on allowing members to communicate with one another—which, after all, is the basis of community. The Dead, by contrast, exerted almost no control over their tribe of fans, instead simply creating an open atmosphere: they worked with venues to allow space for Shakedown Street, an area where fans could sell, buy, and meet up before shows; they allowed fans to communicate with one another through ads in their newsletter; and they tolerated taping, which encouraged peer-to-peer relationships between fans. Beyond that, the Dead let the fans create their own community.

3. Promote values:

Deadheads, following the lead of the band, created a place for themselves within what they saw as the isolation and selfishness of American culture. Just as the band members made a commitment to treat each other, their employees, and their fans with kindness and respect, Deadheads extended the same treatment to one another. The trading of tapes—never sold for cash—was one expression of this ethic of sharing. The same could be said for "miracle tickets," the practice of giving free show tickets to fellow Deadheads who couldn't afford them. Not only tickets but also food, drugs, rides, and clothes were shared freely within the community. Newcomers who tried to scalp tickets or sell tapes were quickly put in their place by seasoned Deadheads. The ethic of caring for one another was extended by a group called Rock Med, a largely volunteer organization that provided emergency medical care at West Coast shows starting in the early 1970s. The group, which generally treated minor issues such as cut feet or heat exhaustion for eighty or so fans a show, described itself as "the Deadheads' HMO." Barlow summarized what made Deadheads a community: "the sense of shared adversity, willingness to take care of each other under duress, economic interdependence—real caring and human contact in a diverse social environment."

A sense of belonging, an open space, a set of values: this is what it takes to foster a community, and the Dead were particularly good at creating the conditions where that could happen. The band wasn't interested simply in producing great music; they wanted to create a way of life for themselves and their audience, and with the collaboration of the Deadheads, they did exactly that. This is why the Deadheads were different from any other group of customers or fans, and why the Dead enjoyed such extraordinary loyalty and longevity.

How the Dead Collaborated with Deadheads

Eric A. Von Hippel, a professor at MIT's Sloan School of Management, has argued that the division between consumers and producers is breaking down, with consumers becoming a major source of innovation. Twitter's popular "Retweet" feature, for instance, was inspired by customer suggestions. And the Internet has made it possible for all types of small-scale inventors—working on everything from software to mountain-climbing equipment—to find each other online and share information. Creativity by consumers, Von Hippel says, is the "new pattern for how innovations come about." The Grateful Dead long ago understood this pattern, forming an intense bond with Deadheads that transcended the relationship of musicians and fans, producers and consumers. What the Dead produced was a meaningful collaboration with their fans, one that anticipated the shape of the business world today.

The origins of the Grateful Dead's deep relationship with its audience can be traced back to the Acid Tests in 1966. Rather than getting paid for their performance, they paid the admission fee like everyone else present. The Dead weren't the entertainment; they were just part of the scene. The Acid Tests were the "template that permanently defined the Grateful Dead's view of its audience," band publicist and historian Dennis McNally has written. "The root basis of their relationship was that of a partnership of equals, of companions in an odyssey." This is very much the spirit of the sixties, a rejection of a hierarchy in which the entertainer and audience were segregated in neatly defined boxes. Even after the Acid Tests ended, and the Dead began to play more conventional shows, they kept the spirit alive. In the early days, the audience was allowed to join the band onstage, dancing and grooving along with the musicians, and throughout their careers the Dead testified to the fact that they simply couldn't be the Dead without the audience. "When it's really happening, the audience is as much the band as the band is the audience. There is no difference," Kreutzmann said. "The audience should be paid—they contribute as much."

Though the Dead have come to be known as a "jam band," they identified themselves, first and foremost, as a dance band. Ralph Gleason, music critic for the *San Francisco Chronicle*, told Garcia in an interview that the interaction between the Dead and the audience hearkened back, surprisingly enough, to the great swing bands of earlier decades. "I've heard the people stomping on the floor," Gleason told Garcia. "I hadn't heard that since the Count Basie bands when they'd take a break and everybody's time was just going right on along. Everybody's in the band!" Garcia agreed: "Right! That's the ideal situation. Everybody should be in the band. And when that's happening, it's really something special. It's an amazing thing."

Everybody should be in the band, and everybody should be in the business. When you erase the distinction between band and audience, between producer and consumer, wonderful things can happen. Ken Kesey once explained the difference between the Dead and other bands: "The Doors were playing at you. John Fogerty was singing at you," he said. Garcia, on the other hand, "was not playing at [the audience]. He was playing with them," and often members of that audience would realize, " 'He's not only moving my mind. My mind is moving him!' " Companies would do well to come to a similar revelation: we're not moving our customers, our customers are moving us!

It was not only more fun and more interesting, it was also more profitable. Because Dead shows were a collaboration between the band and thousands of fans, each concert was unique. Fans understood that if they went to six shows in two weeks, they wouldn't hear six versions of the same show; they'd participate in six completely different concert experiences. By allowing their fans to contribute, the Dead created an astonishing range of shows, and fans returned for more and more. The collaboration created variety, variety increased demand, and demand boosted profits.

How the Dead Put Its Tribe to Work

The Deadheads became a remarkably cohesive, self-sustaining, self-regulating community that was vital to the success of the band. Its only true enemy was success: the band and its culture proved so attractive that they attracted hordes of new fans. In any culture, assimilating new members can be a serious problem. But here the beauty of a good consumer tribe comes into play: when the Deadhead community came under threat, the Deadheads themselves solved the problem. Even more fascinating, the Deadheads organized themselves using the most exciting new technology of the late 1980s: the Internet.

In 1987 the single "Touch of Grey" became a hit on the radio and MTV, and suddenly thousands more people were interested in becoming Deadheads. A cult favorite became a mainstream success, attracting fans who didn't know the ways of the tribe. The Deadhead scene started to draw many more complaints from local officials about drug dealing, drunkenness, public urination, and illegal camping in parks and on residential streets. Neither the Dead nor the Deadheads were responsible for this, but that didn't really matter. The band had begun to attract the bad element, and some cities and venues began banning them. The Dead were in crisis, not so much for fear of loss of revenue but loss of reputation—Deadheads were becoming known as irresponsible and unkind. That's not who they were, and it hurt.

How did the Dead solve this problem? They asked the Deadheads for help. Lyricist Robert Hunter wrote a message that was sent out with every ticket order. "Dear Deadheads: Here we are sitting on top of the world: big record, open doors and lots of steaming plans. This raises the question of who we are—the answer is: partly us, partly you." Hunter here reminds the fans that the Dead are a collaborative effort, demanding attention and adjustment from both sides. "There is no blanket solution to the problems caused by increasing demand, and there is no turning back. We are now the biggest 'draw' in the history of rock 'n' roll. That's not a self-congratulatory statement, rather a bald fact showing the seriousness of our logistical problem. The good old days when we were your personal minstrels have been overshadowed by a new reality which must be addressed. We are not a political, religious nor a grassroots movement; not a counterculture, drug culture nor the latest big shakes snatch-and-run glamour act. We are a symbiotic fun machine."

Symbiotic is the key term. The band needs fans, and fans need the band. So Hunter asked the fans for help, setting up some rules for parking lot vendors, asking fans for patience, and reminding them that "this wasn't meant to be a private party."

Deadheads took up the challenge, using the most democratic of emerging technologies. In 1986 a group of Deadheads had started a Grateful Dead discussion board on an early online community known as "The Well," and it really took off—Deadheads tended to be well educated and affluent, the same demographic that tended to be early adopters of technology. After the problems at Dead shows, the organizers used the online community to recruit those willing to help out at shows, trying to keep the peace and preserve the Deadheads' reputation in the communities where they played. In Oakland they started a group called the Minglewood Town Council (from the song "Minglewood Blues"), who fanned out before and after shows, passing out leaflets and trash bags and asking Deadheads to be respectful of neighbors.

Some problems persisted throughout the band's career, but by the early 1990s the situation had come under control. New fans who cared about the band tended to respond to the entreaties of the Town Council and other organized efforts at self-regulation. More subtle processes of socialization were also at work. After all, a culture grows and adapts because it offers something important to its members: support, meaning, fun, community.

"I think that the word is finally starting to get around," soundman Dan Healy said in June 1991. The message was, as Healy put it, "'Hey if you're a Deadhead, are you causing the world to *not like* Deadheads or are you doing your part to cause the world to *like* Deadheads?' And that's really what it comes down to: Each and every individual in the audience is solely responsible for the collective of all of us and whether or not we are welcome in communities. We all know who we are down inside, but we have to portray that picture outside as well as inside, so that others can see it too. And it's not that hard! Get in a good mood and be a nice person! That's all you gotta do!"

Deadhead culture was strong enough that it could overcome any difficulties. Success didn't destroy the scene; it made it more powerful than ever. Corporations who worry about brand management should take the Dead's example to heart. When the band faced the biggest crisis of its career, police harassment and bans from certain venues and cities, it was the fans who helped solve the problem. If you can nurture the right tribe, it will take care of your brand for you.

Selling Community

In the modern business world, customers and corporations work in collaboration—think open-source software, smartphone apps, or customer reviews on Amazon. As this happens, power is shifting away from companies and flowing toward their customers. People today consume products and services not passively but actively, by "adding to them, grappling with them, blending them with their own lives and altering them," according to the recent book *Consumer Tribes*. Customers today "cannot 'consume' a service without engaging in a dance with the service provider, where the dance becomes the service." In the case of the Grateful Dead and the Deadheads, this was literally true. By dancing to the music, the fans shared in the creation of the band's primary offering, the live concert experience.

The Dead long ago managed to capture the ethos of the Internet age, exploiting its possibilities while skirting its downsides. They collaborated with their fans to create a constantly changing, always unique live-concert experience, and fans responded by buying tickets for dozens or even hundreds of shows, boosting the band's bottom line. The Dead gave control to their fans, and their fans exercised that control responsibly, even using it to solve problems for the band. What accounts for this success?

The Dead created an atmosphere of openness, flexibility, and respect, and their fans responded by creating a tribe based on the same principles. Companies today would do well to try to match the inextricable bond between the Dead and Deadheads.

6

Insource

How the Dead Learned
Do-It-Yourself Business

The Dead, as we've seen, were not afraid of risk. They improvised onstage, in their business offices, and in collaboration with their fans. Their success in these ventures made them bold, and they often came to the conclusion that they could do a job best by doing it themselves. Whereas most rock bands relied heavily on outside vendors and contractors, the Dead did just the opposite: They "insourced," and they benefited enormously in the process.

The trend toward outsourcing—subcontracting certain business functions to an outside firm—really got moving in the 1980s, when Harvard strategy expert Michael Porter developed his "value chain," and management guru

Peter Drucker got on board as well. Now, as so often happens in business theory (and in life!), the pendulum is swinging back the other way. Neither Porter nor Drucker, it should be said, were blind promoters of outsourcing; they simply supported it for those areas in which a company showed no particular talent. And Drucker in particular always made clear that the true goal for any company was not to cut expenses but to boost effectiveness. Many companies learned this lesson the hard way. Boeing's 787 Dreamliner, for instance, fell years behind schedule and went billions over budget in part because of unwise outsourcing agreements with suppliers who weren't up to the challenge. Now many firms are learning they can increase effectiveness by bringing back in-house many functions that had been sent to outside firms. Through direct control, they can oversee an entire process, maintain a high degree of control, and provide more jobs.

The Grateful Dead, in this realm as in so many others, were far ahead of the curve. Most firms today that insource are simply reversing bad outsourcing decisions. The Dead, by contrast, brought in-house a multitude of functions—most prominently a concert venue, a record company, and a ticketing operation—that had almost always been done by outside firms. This proto-insourcing revealed the band's desire to shake up the way business, and particularly the music business, had traditionally been done. This is what Garcia had in mind when he said, at the start of the band's career in 1967,

"We're trying to change the whole atmosphere of music, the business part of it...by dealing with it on a more humanistic level."

The Dead insourced in a truly radical way. Their motivations, though, would sound familiar to any firm that has suffered problems with outsourcing. They found that they could take better care of their employees (by ensuring good jobs), create a higher-quality product (such as records), and provide superior service to their customers (through ticket sales) by doing it themselves rather than counting on outside contractors. Cameron Sears, who became a band employee in 1987, explained how this spirit carried through the band's long career. "When we farmed things out we found that, by that simple fact, we lost control," he said. "And control in the creative process is very important; it's how we maintain our integrity. The more people that come between us and the final delivery of our art, the more diluted it becomes. And the less money we make."

Sears was speaking in 1994, after the Dead's business apparatus had become a well-oiled machine, producing amazing concerts, great records, and solid customer service to fans, while raking in millions upon millions of dollars. It wasn't always that way. Several of the early insourcing ventures flopped, and cost the band money. But the band, as skilled strategic improvisers, learned from these mistakes and eventually figured out how to maintain control and make money.

> **Grateful Dead Business Lesson 6:** Insourcing—bringing as many business functions as possible in-house—increases creative control, keeps customers happier, and boosts profitability.

DIY Concert Hall

The Dead's first experiment in insourcing began in 1968 when they joined together with Jefferson Airplane and Quicksilver Messenger Service to lease the Carousel Ballroom, a San Francisco dance hall. The bands agreed to play for free and receive 10 percent of the profits. It was, in essence, an attempt to bypass the middlemen of promoters and hall rentals, and enjoy all the benefits themselves. The biggest player in this arrangement was the Airplane, who at the time pulled down $7,500 a show, the most for any band in the nation.

As it happened, the venture was doomed from the start by a bad contract. The project was headed up by Ron Rakow, a former Wall Street trader and favorite of Garcia's, who was big on charm but, according to some, short on business sense. He signed a terrible lease for the Carousel, $7,000 a month *plus* 15 percent of the gross from each show. He later claimed his lawyer had made a mistake, that it should have been $7,000 *against* 15 percent.

Whoever's fault it was, the lease was signed, and the bands quickly discovered that the terms were crippling. Bill Thompson, manager for the Airplane, said, "We got ten percent. Ten percent of nothing." After a few months, the finances caught up with them, and Bill Graham assumed control of the hall and renamed it the Fillmore West, under which name it became a legendary rock club.

Though a failure as a business venture, the Carousel was a success by other measures. It functioned as not just a music venue but also a sort of community center, where the Black Panthers and other groups kept offices. "People who cared about each other and loved what they were doing came together" at the Carousel, Dennis McNally said; those people thus turned it into "a sanctuary and an experiment in community." It was a grand social experiment, which, after all, was what the Dead were all about.

Even more important, the members of the band's extended family were learning how to work together as a business. Jon McIntire, an actor and history student, volunteered to help clean the kitchen at the Carousel and ended up running the concessions. He had no regrets about the Carousel, describing it as "four months of the greatest, loosest thing that ever, to my knowledge, happened anywhere." McIntire, from his start in the Carousel's filthy kitchen, would go on to become one of the Dead's most important managers. And the wisdom he brought was forged in episodes like the Carousel.

The Carousel provided an important trial by fire in the

world of entertainment business. Ultimately, the Dead may have made more money had they continued in the familiar pattern of working with promoters and being paid a fee or a percentage for each show. But the lessons they learned from this insourcing experiment turned out to be far more valuable than any lost revenue. First, they learned that by being in control, they could express their values through the operation, by offering offices to community groups. Second, insourcing increased the number of people they needed to hire, and thus served as a valuable training ground for important future employees. Third, the venture gave important business training for the band members themselves, teaching them about concert promotion, gate receipts, and legal contracts. If they wanted to change the music business, they needed to understand it in detail. Only through insourcing, through running the operation themselves, could they get the understanding—and eventually the economic clout—they needed.

DIY Record Making

The Grateful Dead's experiment in the record business extended the lesson they'd learned at the Carousel, teaching them both the benefits and the dangers of going it alone. By disrupting the old habits of the rock 'n' roll business, they opened a new space for creativity.

The Dead always had an uneasy relationship with record companies, starting with their first deal—they signed with Warner Bros. in 1966, earning a $10,000 advance and an 8 percent royalty. The relationship with the record label, though, was far from happy. The Dead's first three records—*The Grateful Dead* (1967), *Anthem of the Sun* (1968), and *Aoxomoxoa* (1969)—sold poorly, and the band ran up a lot of debt to Warner Bros., mostly from extended stays in the recording studio. When the band was slow in recording *Anthem of the Sun*, they got a nasty letter from Joe Smith at Warner Bros., who called it "the most unreasonable project with which we have ever involved ourselves" and upbraided the band members for "lack of preparation, direction and cooperation" and "lack of professionalism." With debts mounting, the band came under increasing pressure from the record company to produce hits. It didn't work out. "All that pressure to make commercial records more or less drew a backlash from us," Weir said in 1987. "We just lost interest."

The Dead, of course, weren't interested in being professional, at least if that meant controlling costs—they placed a far greater value on the authenticity of their music than on the efficiency of their business. They spent a lot of time in the studio because they wanted to make a record their way. If Warner Bros. didn't like that, tough luck. By 1969, the band had run up a debt to the label of $180,000. Fortunately, the next album they put out, *Live Dead* (1969), was brilliant, sold well, and rescued the relationship. Things improved further with *Workingman's Dead*, their most accessible record to date, and *American Beauty*, which also sold well. Another live album, *Grateful Dead* (aka *Skullfuck* or *Skull and Roses*) came next and became their first gold record.

As Warner Bros. became happier with the Dead's output, however, the Dead became more dissatisfied with Warner Bros. Garcia had this to say of the label in 1973: "We were never satisfied with the whole trip and having to deal with people we couldn't relate to." Like the rest of the band, he felt that Warner Bros. values didn't align with those of the Dead. And since values were so important to the band, this mismatch became a significant problem.

So did the simple quality of the work the label was doing. Ron Rakow conducted a test: he sent the band's tour itinerary to Warner Bros. three weeks in advance, and asked them to make sure record stores in those cities were stocked, on the theory, he said, that "records really move when the band is in town." Then, when the band got to St. Louis, Rakow checked the record store and found the bins empty, and "that's what happened, store after store, city after city.... They [Warner Bros.] did shit, period." Warner Bros., like a lot of established companies, had simply become complacent. Because the Dead were locked into a contract, the label didn't feel the need to give them full attention. As a result, the Dead exercised their right to walk away.

When the Warner Bros. contract expired in December 1972, the band decided to go it alone by creating Grateful Dead Records. As Garcia explained, "Even if we fucked up real bad, we could still sell as many records as Warner Bros. could." It was a bold step, one that no other major act had undertaken. The Beatles, the Rolling Stones, and the Jefferson Airplane officially had their own labels, but as one music critic explained, such labels were "just ego-boosting scraps of paper representing a little bit more economic and artistic clout. All the real work a record company does still belongs to the media conglomerates—RCA, MCA, Warner-Atlantic, Capitol. Those are the organizations which press and distribute, market and bill the accounts for the records of even these private-stock labels." The Dead, by contrast, would have no ties with any record company, and they would take on all these responsibilities themselves.

Insourcing record production allowed the Dead to:

- Exert more control over business practices: They were cautious in determining how many records to press and carefully analyzed the sales of the Warner Bros. albums in each of the distributor areas. Their distribution deal minimized unsold returns, which were a common problem in the record business. They allowed no returns on the initial order, had their distributors pay up front through First National Bank of Boston, and sold the albums at a slightly lower price than other record companies.

- Cut ties with companies whose practices they didn't approve of: The Dead believed record companies put too much focus on commercialism rather than high-quality music. As Garcia explained, Grateful Dead Records was "designed to sell our records in a way compatible with the way we run our scene." That is, it was focused on treating employees and fans with respect.

- Keep a larger share of the take: Though Garcia said the company was not "designed for profit," that's not to say the record company wasn't intended to make money. They just wanted the money to flow back to the band, in order to ease the demands of their touring schedule while still covering their big overhead for personal and innovation costs. According to Rakow, he sold the record company idea to Garcia by telling him, "The record industry does nothing for the Grateful Dead. It's the other way round. The Grateful Dead should sell its own products through its own fans and make more money and support its own people as opposed to those who don't admire them."

- Lower record prices for fans: Garcia explained that given the band's bigger percentage, "We can also afford to lower the prices."

- Improve the manufacturing quality of its records: Weir had been particularly unhappy with the physical product Warner Bros. was putting out. Once, he put a brand-new Dead record on his turntable and "the needle zipped all the way across the record without playing a note," he said, exasperated. "They were going to sell this thing. I knew then that we couldn't tolerate much more of this." To avoid this, Grateful Dead Records sent representatives to supervise the quality control in the four pressing plants, where the vinyl was stamped into LP records. This was the most technical side of the record business, and it remained mysterious to almost all musicians. The Dead, however, did their homework and went to the plants with detailed specifications. "They knew not only what kind of vinyl alloy they wanted, but also the manufacturer who made it," says publicist Barbara Christenson. And to ensure that this high-quality vinyl was used to its best advantage, the band directed the pressing plant to toss out the "mothers"—the master copies that made the actual impressions onto the vinyl—after 500 copies instead of the usual 1,400 to 1,500. This was far more expensive, but it meant the last copy made from each mother was of nearly as high a quality as the first. A mainstream record company, focused on shorter-term profits, never would have made this decision. But for the Dead, who were focused on building long-term relationships with fans, it made sense.

- Increase connection with fans: The Grateful Dead Records provided higher returns on record sales, and this allowed the band to create a budget for mailings to their fan club. Newsletters went out two or three times a year, with tour information and notes from the musicians. This effort built the foundation for the Dead's spectacularly loyal fan base, and, as we've seen, set the groundwork for the band's pioneering efforts in database marketing. They even used the power of this mailing list to promote the success of the record label itself. The newsletter urged fans to "joyously and systematically make sure, by repeated gentle motions and phone calls, that every record dealer knows that our records have to be in plain view." The letter also urged fans to "put up the posters, stickers, and hand-bills... [and] call radio stations."

The first LP for Grateful Dead Records, *Wake of the Flood*, was released in October 1973 and sold 400,000 copies, a 15 percent gain over their last album with Warner Bros. Thanks to their higher percentage, it also was vastly more profitable. The next LP, *Grateful Dead from the Mars Hotel*, which was released only ten months later, in June 1974, sold only 238,000 copies and received bad reviews. And then it got worse. An expensive movie project financially crippled the band. Rakow began clashing with band members, and ultimately was fired. He decided not to go quietly. He cut himself a check for $225,000. It was money he said he was owed, but others on the scene disagreed. Garcia eventually negotiated a deal in which

Rakow kept the cash but gave up any financial interest in the record company. Whatever Rakow's right to that money, taking it at that point was a cruel blow, crippling the company. It folded in the summer of 1976.

The record company, by standard measures of business, was a failure. As always, though, the Dead learned from their errors. The band now knew the details of record pressing, promotion, and distribution, which helped them in later dealings with outside record companies. Even more important, it gave them the incentive to build their mailing list and improve their fan network. What started as an outlet for record sales became something far more vital and gave the Dead the confidence they would need for their next adventure in insourcing.

DIY Ticket Sales

In the fall of 1980, the Dead celebrated their fifteenth anniversary with fifteen shows at the Warfield, a theater in San Francisco, and eight shows at Radio City Music Hall in New York. So many kids camped out outside Radio City that it stopped the flow of people into Rockefeller Center. Once the ticket office opened, only a handful could buy tickets. The rest of the tickets, according to band employee Nicki Scully, "had all been pre-scalped." This wasn't the only problem with Dead tickets. In the early 1980s, the Ticketmaster era of mass ticket sales via telephone—much less Internet—had not yet arrived. Acquiring tickets to see the Dead required standing in line at a ticket office, and given the devotion of Dead fans, this usually meant spending a night on the sidewalk. For some fans, this was just part of the experience. But, as McNally notes, "there were committed Deadheads with jobs who could not spare the time."

In response, the Dead created an in-house ticketing operation, Grateful Dead Ticket Sales. This was paired with a telephone hotline offering recorded information about upcoming tours and special events. Eventually there would be two hotlines, one for each coast, and a third number for problems with tickets. Deadheads now could determine when and where the Dead would be playing next and obtain tickets, usually a month or more before they went on sale at the local venue. As McNally put it, "it proved to be a marvelous idea, not only because it employed dozens of family members but also because it opened up the demographics of the audience to include people with more or less conventional lives. The hardest core would always find a way, but now the respectable could too."

They didn't accomplish this insourcing without a fight. Ticketmaster, which had been founded in 1976, had signed exclusive contracts with most of the venues where the Dead played. Conflict was inevitable. At a meeting, Ticketmaster officials told Dead lawyer Hal Kant that the Dead's in-house ticket operations interfered with Ticketmaster's business. Kant, always on his toes, threatened to sue Ticketmaster, charging that the Dead's relationships with these venues predated Ticketmaster, and therefore Ticketmaster had interfered with the Dead's contractual relations with the venues. They reached a settlement, and the Dead got to continue selling tickets. Over the next decade, in-house ticket sales grew from 24,500 the first year to 115,000 annually in the 1990s. By cutting out the middleman, they were able to keep a higher proportion of ticket revenue, and thereby keep prices lower. At a time when other rock 'n' roll legends such as the Rolling Stones were attracting corporate sponsorship to their tours and raising ticket prices to astronomical levels, the Dead put a ceiling of thirty dollars on ticket prices, and they never accepted corporate sponsorships.

The Dead was the only band to make a success of such a complex operation. As always with them, it wasn't just about money. Insourcing the ticket sales not only made things easier for Deadheads with jobs, made the band more money, and helped keep ticket prices lower, but it also made the Dead's relationship with fans more intimate. The fans sent order forms and checks, and they got tickets in return. Instead of dealing with a box office, they were dealing directly with the Dead.

And it became very personal indeed. When they requested tickets, fans would send in envelopes often elaborately decorated with Grateful Dead–style artwork— either to heighten their chances of being granted tickets, or simply as a small gift to the Grateful Dead, a thank-you for the musical joy the Dead had brought them. The Dead reciprocated, adding artwork to the tickets, different for each concert, making each ticket even more of a memento of the event. Tickets for New Year's Eve shows, always an important date on the Dead calendar, evolved over the years into spectacular pieces of art. What had started out as a straight financial exchange—tickets for money—became something much deeper, and drew the Dead and their fans closer together.

The Value of Bringing It Home

In the 1960s the Dead had general disdain for the business world. They were convinced that if they worked only with people they knew and trusted, they could avoid some negative aspects of doing business: too much emphasis on profits, a lack of concern for others, power concentrated at the top of the hierarchy, and a limited understanding of customer needs and wants. The Dead "pursue a direction of self-determination in as many ways as interestingly possible, believing that this course will best aid a continuation of integrity and meaning in their music and other life spaces," said longtime band employee Willy Legate. "This has meant that their business activity seeks to be in control of as many areas as become possible, employing their own people to do the work that would otherwise be farmed out to straight business. Thus there is the possibility that the message in the music can be reflected in the manner and purpose of conducting the business necessary to get the music heard."

As we've seen, it didn't always work, but these failures laid the groundwork for future success. From the Carousel, the band learned how to put on live shows, and the intricacies of record pressing, distribution, and promotion, skills that would help them as they moved ahead with outside providers of these services. Even more important, the record company venture brought them into direct contact with their fans, which allowed them to build up a mailing list and interact directly with their customers. They also built up a staff with an increasing level of commitment and business acumen. When it came time to launch Grateful Dead Ticket Sales, they knew what they were doing, and they had the access to their fans they needed to make it work. Their deep commitment to putting out well-made records and to providing great customer service paid off in the end.

It goes without saying that no business should outsource a core competence, because giving up control of your distinctive advantage would be the height of folly. The Grateful Dead, though, expanded on this concept, using insourcing to move beyond their first core competence, playing music, into customer service and direct sales. By bringing ticketing and merchandising functions in-house, the band expanded its business plan and its capacity to please customers and make sales.

The recent mania for the opposite business principle, outsourcing, was driven by a desire to save money, provide better services through specialized firms, and manage staffing levels more efficiently. For many companies, this worked. Others, though, found that the services provided by the other firms proved lower in quality because the people doing the work had less knowledge of the company and less commitment to the core mission. There's still a case to be made for many sorts of outsourcing—indeed, in many industries you can't be competitive without it. In today's climate, however, every aspect of a business's operation is scrutinized by savvy consumers who ask questions about labor practices, environmental health, and human rights, in addition to demanding personalized customer service. The Dead proved that insourcing works and that a great business can be built by going it alone.

7

Innovate Constantly

How the Dead Stayed
on the Cutting Edge

A woman once asked Jerry Garcia, "What do you think about somebody who spends all his money going to Grateful Dead concerts?"

Garcia's answer: "What the hell do you think we do?" He was quite serious.

Until the band hit the mainstream in 1987, having enough money was never guaranteed. In addition to its high staffing costs, the band spent a fortune on technology, not just off-the-shelf items but also custom-built instruments, recording equipment, and, especially, sound systems. Unlike most rock bands, the Grateful Dead wanted their shows to be not merely loud but also precise—to blow listeners away with subtlety as well as power. When they discovered they couldn't buy such equipment, they worked to develop the technology themselves. None of this came cheap, but the band members decided that the normal way just wasn't good enough. They innovated relentlessly, regardless of the cost, to provide the best possible experience for their customers.

To stay ahead, a business must keep reinventing itself, keep working to change things for the better. In some cases, this means borrowing best practices from other companies. But to be innovative means doing things no one else is doing, even if this means doing the seemingly impossible, and departing from convention in stunning ways to transform an industry. Take, for example, Tata Motors, the Indian auto company that decided to go back to the drawing board, challenging parts suppliers and its own engineers to rethink every component in order to cut costs and minimize weight. When challenged by Tata, the parts supplier Delphi created an instrument cluster weighing just fourteen ounces, about a third of the standard. Another supplier created an unusual single-windshield wiper to trim costs and weight further. The result was an inexpensive, fuel-efficient yet solid automobile—pointing the way toward the future of the global car market.

Unlike Tata, the Dead weren't interested in smaller and cheaper—they tended to gravitate toward larger and more expensive. Yet they resembled Tata in one clear sense: their willingness to toss out the playbook and demand that their engineers produce something entirely new. And as with all top companies, the ultimate goal was the same: keeping customers happy. "Instead of buying yachts and Riviera condos and that sort of shit, the Dead have always poured money back into the scene in the form of sound and lights and musical instruments," said Dan Healy, the band's legendary soundman. And they did it for the fans: "Of all the things that we've done—and Lord knows we're probably guilty of everything known—we've never been un-loyal to our music and our audience," Healy said. "Even in our deepest, darkest moments, when there was probably an easier way out, we didn't take the easy way out."

Businesses too often fail by taking the easy way out, sticking with the tried-and-true rather than taking a leap into the unknown. To survive and grow, businesses must innovate continually, even when—especially when—that innovation carries a high risk of failure. The willingness to disrupt old habits and to take risks will make your business successful and your workers nimble and adaptable.

Grateful Dead Business Lesson 7: Innovate constantly, despite risks of failure and financial loss, in order to keep your business ahead of the curve.

Hitting the Wall

When the Dead first tried to improve their amplified sound, they ran into a problem: there weren't many equipment makers in the market. Before rock music became widespread, most amplifiers were purchased by theaters and dance halls, whose needs were very different. As Clayton Christensen explained in his pioneering book *The Innovator's Dilemma*, established firms can be held captive by their current customers—they're so comfortable serving an established market that they miss out on opportunities to pioneer a truly disruptive technology that will create new markets. This leaves a space for new players to take over.

These days, when even teenage garage bands have good sound equipment, it's easy to forget how primitive things were when the Dead started playing in the mid-1960s. Monitors—the speakers musicians use to hear themselves—had not been invented. Smaller venues, such as the In Room, where the band had their first regular gig, had no sound systems at all, and instrument amplifiers provided the only sound. If a concert venue did have a public address system, it was designed for singers and speakers, not electric instruments. Drummers generally weren't amplified at all. Singers plugged their mikes into an instrument amp and did their best to sing as loudly as they were playing. Mixing was crude at best—the volumes of the various instrument amps were adjusted to create some sort of balance. Such technology could be adequate, if barely, at small clubs, but at larger venues, especially those with high ceilings, the situation was ugly.

The Dead's own amps sufficed for their earliest pizza parlor gigs in 1965, but their exploding fan base pushed them into larger venues. At dance halls and theaters, they were dismayed by the low quality of the sound they were offering their fans. "The thing to do, obviously, when you play in a big hall, is to make it so that you can hear everything everywhere," Garcia told an interviewer during this period. But when they took the obvious step and cranked up the volume, they lost definition. "It's more important that it be clear than loud," Garcia said, adding, "It would be nice if it were both loud and clear."

The first person to take charge of the Dead's efforts to be "loud and clear" was Owsley "Bear" Stanley, the Acid King of California. Bear was the grandson of a former U.S. senator and governor from Kentucky, but he was also an amateur chemist who had turned himself into one of the world's major producers of high-quality LSD. He fell in love with the Dead, but he thought the available musical technology was holding them back. "In the days of Bach, the highest, most technologically superb things that were being built were the great organs. Music was the height of technology," Bear recalled. In the 1960s, though, America was "building rockets that could deliver atomic bombs to destroy entire cities, and musicians were playing on something that looked like it was built in a garage in the 1930s....Nobody seemed to care. I figured it was worth caring about."

In the 1960s, rock music carried enormous social significance, providing the rituals for a newly created youth culture, but the technology wasn't up to snuff. Bear's reference to Bach and organs may sound overblown, but he was onto something true: the technology hadn't caught up to the culture. A decade later, in the 1970s, the Sony Walkman would capture a technological moment focused on fitness and private experience. But the '60s was about communal experience, about shared sound, about music so loud it frightened the old people. What Bear saw was a space available for innovation. What Bear had recognized, in his offbeat way, was a tremendous gap in the market. So he worked to fill it.

Pursuing his goal of a sound system that was transparent, clear, undistorted, and very loud, Bear bankrolled the Dead's experiments in musical technology. He had some background in electronics, but what he really offered was a commitment to perfection. The same quality that made him an expert LSD chemist allowed him to build some pioneering amplification equipment. With the help of a young electronics genius named Tim Scully, he began to look into ways of developing a good sound system that could hold up to the bashing about that came from being carried from van to stage and back again many times a week. At first they tried to work with Altec Lansing, a major player in the industry, to develop a more powerful system, but they were unresponsive. Bear recalled an Altec rep saying, "We're not interested. Besides, we sell all the speakers we make anyway. Get lost!" This is the classic innovator's dilemma: an establishment player hampered by commitments to current clients.

Rebuffed by the PA industry's biggest companies, Bear and Scully set out to build a system of their own. Urged on by Bear, Scully used his electronics knowledge to create a rudimentary central preamp and mixing system. This central mixing box created a number of new opportunities: first, Bear began recording stereo tapes of the band's performances (a fact that would be crucial to the band's recording legacy); second, it allowed the band to use monitors, so they could hear themselves play more accurately and make appropriate adjustments; finally, the box had a preamp for each instrument, which allowed for more precise mixing.

The system was a technological marvel, and produced some of the cleanest, most powerful sound of any rock 'n' roll band. Unfortunately, it tended to break. Not infrequently the band would be ready to play, only to find Bear on the floor fiddling with equipment. At a benefit for the Hell's Angels, Bear was still soldering well past the scheduled start time, "and there were these six-foot Hell's Angels coming up and saying, 'Uh, you think you

could play some music?'" musical colleague John Dawson recalled. "We were saying, 'Bear, *come on*. Get this
goddamn thing *fixed*.'" After a disastrous trip to California in the summer of 1966, the band gave Bear's system the heave-ho. He sold it off and gave the money to
the band to buy some regular old Fender amps.

It was a retreat, of sorts, but the experiment was not
in vain. Bear inspired the band to think about "the inad-
equacy of the prevailing live sound systems of the day,
while pointing at possibilities for improving the state of
the art," according to Dead expert Blair Jackson. And
this is the reason for technological innovation. You might
fail, but you get a clearer vision of the future.

Start from Scratch

As the sixties turned into the seventies, the Dead's audience was growing, and they needed to play bigger venues to satisfy demand for tickets. Those bigger venues,
of course, demanded bigger and better sound systems.
In 1968 the band had hooked up with a recording
expert named Ron Wickersham, who had been working for Ampex, a maker of high-end recording and mixing equipment. Rather than becoming a Dead employee,
Wickersham founded a company called Alembic, which
for years would have the Dead as its main customer. Bear
had already modified most of the band's instruments,

and Alembic took over that work, designing guitars and basses to the musicians' specifications. It also took on the band's sound systems, modified the existing components, and then created new ones from scratch—stage boxes, cabinets, horns, monitors, cables.

In 1972 Wickersham decided to address the issue of poor sound at large venues by creating a "PA Consulting Committee," whose members included Wickersham, Bear, and soundman Dan Healy. A recording studio expert, Healy had been with the band for several years, and he would become a mainstay at the band's mixing boards for more than two decades. Wickersham, Healy, and Bear would become the core of the band's sound system brain trust. "The Dead kept playing bigger and bigger venues, and the house or rented sound systems kept sounding worse and worse," said Wickersham. "So we tried to break it all down and address every area we could, because it wasn't like there was a single thing wrong with the instruments, microphones or recording gear, the live PA, and all that. It was a constant fight to try to get *every* detail better."

Like Tata Motors, the Dead had to start from scratch. Sound systems for electric music were extraordinarily complex and little understood, so this wasn't an undertaking that could be done piecemeal. Moreover, the Dead instituted a classic team approach to innovation, with more than a half dozen people contributing ideas. As Wickersham explained, "We were fiercely critical of what was there, and we drove to improve it, together." The existing scientific knowledge about amplified music dated to Bell Labs in the 1920s and '30s, and it wasn't good enough. "Technology had to change," Healy said. And since no one else was making it, "it became a matter of us developing the technology ourselves."

Alembic, with guidance from Bear and Healy, began building a vast array of equipment for the band, everything from a new type of microphone to a new PA array to heavily modified instruments. And Bear was a stickler for detail. "Everything that went on in the sound system had to be paid attention to," Wickersham said. "He was hypercritical about building mic cables, how to coil up the mic cables; every detail. You respected every piece of gear." Like every great innovator, Bear understood that the smallest, least glamorous component could be a key to an entire system.

Such attention to detail was crucial in the enormous system they created, which came to be known as the Wall of Sound. The problems it needed to address were enormous. Indoors, the bass sounds bounced around the walls and interfered with subsequent notes; outdoors, the bass spread into the sky and disappeared. If you ran more than one instrument through the same speakers, you got distortion. The Wall of Sound was designed to fix these problems and more. It consisted of 604 speakers drawing 26,400 watts of power from 55 amplifiers of 600 watts. But it wasn't simply a matter of size. Each instrument had its own column of speakers, with a cluster in the center of the stage for vocals. There were nine separate channels, which means each vocal and instrument had its own feed, thus eliminating distortion. The Dead's newsletter explained the system to fans: "No two musical 'voices' go through the same system. Thus the vocals, piano, drums, lead guitar, rhythm guitar, and bass each have their own channel of amplification. This separation is designed to produce an undistorted sound." The system could deliver quality sound a quarter of a mile away—crucial for outdoor and stadium shows.

The mockumentary *This Is Spinal Tap* contains the famous joke about amps being "turned up to eleven." The Wall of Sound was so powerful that it was rarely turned past two. As Healy put it, "You could get it amazingly loud, and it was amazingly clean." The band finally could achieve the sound Garcia had dreamed about back in 1967—"loud and clear."

The Wall of Sound also allowed the band to fulfill its mission of perfect harmony with the audience. Because the Wall acted as its own monitor system, there was no need for the usual barrier of speakers at the front of the stage to allow band members to hear what they were playing. With the speakers behind the band, the musicians heard exactly what the audience was hearing. They were, as Owsley described it, "embedded in that sound field." This meant the musicians could hear and control every element of the concert. They were their own sound mixers, which blended perfectly with the band's philosophy. For years Lesh and Owsley had discussed what they called microcosm and macrocosm, the world of the stage and the world of the audience. The goal was to blend those two seamlessly into one. "All the control of what's going to the audience should be fully in the hands of the performing artists themselves," Owsley later explained. Here, then, was a perfect technology, allowing the worker to do his job in the best way possible.

There was just one problem: it was utterly impractical.

The result of eight years of experimentation, the Wall of Sound cost an estimated $350,000 to develop, an enormous sum in those days. And while manufacturing companies spread out their R&D expenses over the run of the product, the Dead were inventing, from scratch, a one-off system. They couldn't recapture their expenses by selling versions to other people. Adding to the expense were the logistics. There were, in fact, *two* Walls of Sound. It took two days to install and test the Wall at each venue, so the only way to mount a normal tour was to have one system in use while the other was being trucked to the next city. When the Wall first went on tour in May 1974, the Grateful Dead hit the road with four trucks, six band members, ten people for crew and sound, four more for lights, seven for stages and trucking, and three for management. The convoy traveled far, to Iowa, Montana, British Columbia, and to standard spots on the coasts and in the Midwest and South. It even traveled to seven shows in Europe.

Overhead rose to $100,000 a month, which meant the band was struggling to break even. "We had pretty much roped ourselves into an unworkable situation," Bob Weir explained. "Every time we played somewhere we lost money, but we had to keep on working just to pay everybody who was on salary.... Millions and millions of dollars went into that. It wasn't any fun after a while, not having enough time to really get loose and get creative, having to stay on the road all the time. So we decided that we had to knock it off."

After ending their touring in the fall of 1974, the Dead went on hiatus for eighteen months. The Wall of Sound was broken up—some parts kept by the band, some sold, most of it given away to other bands in need. Its legacy, though, would live on. As strategic improvisers, the Dead would learn from this expensive mistake.

After the Wall

The band members spent their year-and-a-half hiatus in 1975–76 recuperating, writing music, and recording. The layoff reminded them how much they loved touring, so they resumed in a pared-back style. They rented their sound systems—more modest affairs, but still with excellent quality. They combined two rented systems that mimicked the performance of the Wall at a much lower price. After renting from Bill Graham's production company for a while, in 1978 the Dead switched over to the major East Coast company Clair Brothers, famous for their quality equipment. Upon testing the rented equipment, though, Healy discovered that nearly a third of the speakers were improperly maintained, producing subpar sound. Clair Brothers, embarrassed, made sure they did better quality control after that. And the Dead's deep experience with building their own sound systems paid another dividend: the ability to evaluate the equipment they rented.

By the 1980s the band's equipment included a harmonic analyzer (priced at $30,000 and created by NASA to test the strength of metals), steel-jacketed NASA surplus cables, and 144 Meyer Sound Lab loudspeakers. By the 1990s they had a $3.5-million computer-assisted sound system. More impressive than the equipment, though, was the technical knowledge devoted to improving the sound. Before a tour, they collected architectural drawings of each venue and scanned them into the architectural design program AutoCAD, using the software to design the perfect configuration of speakers to match the shape of the hall. The software would spit out a blueprint for the crew, and when they got to the venue, they'd have a perfectly tailored plan for creating a sound system. After the tour, they'd do a postmortem on each performance, store up the information on aspects of each venue, and apply the lessons the next time they played there. Because weather can affect sound at outdoor shows, Healy tracked atmospheric conditions and adjusted the system to compensate. At the end of the tour, each piece of equipment was dismantled, cleaned, tested, and repaired—a month-long process after each tour.

Through the end of their careers, the Dead were famous for offering one of the greatest sonic experiences in rock 'n' roll, and much of that was a legacy of the Wall of Sound. By building their own system from scratch, Bear, Healy, and others advanced the state of the art and gained the knowledge necessary to get crystalline sound from whatever system they were using.

Risk It

In nearly everything they did, the Grateful Dead were concerned above all with the authenticity of their music and the experience they gave their fans. When the band's popularity pushed them into larger venues, both of those values were at stake: because existing audio technology wasn't up to the task, the music and the audience experience suffered, so they chose to invest, and to invest big.

The Wall of Sound was the most dramatic, expensive, and forward-looking of the Dead's technological innovations, but it was far from the only one. Consider, for example, Lesh's Alembicized Guild Starfire bass, also known as "The Godfather" and "Big Brown," which had a quadraphonic pickup (with a dedicated channel for each string) and *fourteen* knobs that controlled bandwidth, frequency response, resonance, and filtering. Or his Mission Control bass, which featured improved electronics and cost in the neighborhood of $30,000—and that's in 1973 dollars. It was innovations like these that allowed the band's instruments to be as loud and clear—not to mention weird—as the sound system.

What's more, the Dead kept their fans in the loop, explaining exactly what they were doing. In a 1974 Deadhead newsletter, the band revealed that eighteen cents of every "Grateful Dead Dollar" was spent on equipment purchases and maintenance, explaining that "the physics of sound projection dictate that any given increase in the size of a hall requires exponential rate of increase in equipment capability to reach everyone in the hall with quality at volume." In other words, it was all about the fans, and the Dead really meant that.

The Wall of Sound offered a quantum leap in sound technology, and it showed an extraordinary devotion to their fans and to their art. "I still consider it the best large-venue live sound performance system that has ever existed," Bear said. The Wall "did what it was supposed to do," Healy said. "It completely scrapped and rewrote the rules."

For comparison, we might look at another failed but influential venture, the NeXT Computer developed by

Steve Jobs after he was forced to resign from Apple. A computer aimed at the university and business markets, NeXT sold only about fifty thousand units. Its approach to computing, however—relying on object-oriented programming and graphical user interfaces—proved highly influential in the development of future operating systems from Apple and other software makers.

Also, the experience Jobs gained at NeXT proved invaluable when he returned to Apple and once again upended the computer industry. In designing the iPad, Apple's revolutionary touch-screen tablet, the company was dissatisfied with the available processors, which serve as the guts of the device. Unwilling to partner with a chip supplier such as Intel, Apple decided to develop its own multifunction chip, known as the A4. By doing so, it was able to make the iPad both very speedy and very frugal with power—an ideal combination for its customers. With its iPad chip, Apple hit a home run on its first swing. The Dead were not so lucky, and perhaps not so savvy (after all, they were a band and not a technology company). What matters, though, is that they were willing to keep trying, to keep investing, to keep innovating.

The Dead had an extraordinary appetite for risk. "We were so fortunate that we had the Dead," Wickersham, of Alembic, said of the Dead's investment in the Wall of Sound. "It wouldn't have happened without them. They were always willing to spend the money." Healy illustrated the band's attitude toward technology investment by telling a story about a show at Stanford University where he was testing pricey new high-frequency drivers. "Something went wrong and I turned it on and it just fried all these things in about two seconds. It was like fifteen thousand dollars, whoops, out the window," he explained. But it didn't worry the Dead. "All they did was pick me up and say, 'Go for it again,'" Healy said. "When you're in the process of cultivating new information and you're charting territories yet uncharted, there's no guarantee that it's going to be safe. It's probably just as well, because you have to be really serious to get there."

"Charting territories yet uncharted": that's what the Dead did, in technology as in music. A few spectacular shipwrecks were inevitable, but the band always rebuilt and kept exploring. This willingness to take big risks, to win some and lose some and then move on to the next challenge, is crucial to strategic improvisation—and especially to bold innovation.

8

Transform Through Leadership

How Jerry Garcia Inspired
Greatness in the Dead

The Grateful Dead's organizational chart contained an apparent paradox: Jerry Garcia always denied he was the group's leader, and everyone else insisted he was.

Here's Garcia in 1972: "I'm not the leader of the Grateful Dead or anything like that. There isn't any... leader. I don't think you need it anymore because everybody is the leader."

On the other hand, band manager Jon McIntire had this to say: "At the really big junctures, Garcia called the shots."

What may at first appear to be a paradox, though, is nothing of the sort.

Was Jerry Garcia a leader? Yes.

What type of leader was he? The type of leader who denies leadership and becomes all the more influential as a result. Garcia mastered the art of "transformational leadership," the ability to inspire greatness and bring about profound change. As the business theorist Peter Northouse has explained, transformational leaders do their work through charisma (acting as strong role models), inspiration (motivating others to emulate their high standards), stimulation (encouraging creativity), and individualized coaching (teasing out top performances from each member of the team). The transformational leader looks to the future, and challenges the other workers to do the same. Thus motivated, workers look out for one another, and for the good of the organization. The transformational leader inspires followers to "produce far beyond what is expected of them."

This was Garcia's leadership style: improving the performance of those around him and inspiring greatness in the entire organization. Onstage, the Dead were "transformed from ordinary players to extraordinary ones," Garcia once said, while "the audience wants to be transformed from whatever ordinary reality they may be in to something a little wider, something that enlarges them." While performing and helping run the Dead's business enterprises, Garcia was never happy with the status quo, always looking for new and better ways to do things. It was his vision of continual improvement that inspired the Wall of Sound and Grateful Dead Ticket Sales. He encouraged the band to work together, overcome difficulties, and carry on in their vision of producing a constantly improving musical experience for their fans. He instituted a culture of continual improvement and transformation, one that allowed the organization (though not the band itself) to survive his death and prosper in a new era.

> **Grateful Dead Business Lesson 8:** Transformational leaders create cohesiveness in an organization and inspire others to achieve greatness.

Count on Charisma

Jerry Garcia's leadership potential was obvious to nearly everyone who came in contact with him. Suzy Wood, who knew Garcia from the early 1960s scene in Palo Alto, recognized his greatness early on. "Even though Jerry was a dropout, because of the kind of intelligence and charm and insight that he had, he always seemed more like a leader than a bad guy," she said. "My dad thought he was a wonderful person but he'd say, 'Why doesn't he *do* something with his life?'" It's a telling quotation. Garcia sat on the cusp of great cultural change. He was obviously a leader, but his cause—creating great music—was not yet recognized as worthy. David Nelson, a musician who played with Garcia in the early years, recalls that Garcia possessed "something awesome, some invisible quality." Alan Trist, who also met Garcia around this time, recalls similar feelings the first time he sat with him: "His charisma was really attractive." Sue Stephens, a longtime band employee, recalls that during the band's 1978 trip to Egypt, authorities always singled him out for drug searches because they just assumed he was in charge: "They totally zeroed in on him—not knowing who he was as far as a rock star or anything. He drew that kind of attention. He was just that kind of person. I think his molecules were more dense than most people's."

A couple of years before joining the band, Bill Kreutzmann saw Garcia play a live show and said to himself, "God, I'm going to follow Jerry forever." What Kreutzmann and the others recognized was the first quality of the transformational leader: the charisma that makes people want to fall into ranks and follow you. Charisma, for people like Garcia, seems to be an innate quality, and in that respect it is the hardest aspect of leadership to teach. Businesses, though, can still draw useful lessons from Garcia's example. First, they should remember that the power of charismatic leaders to inspire greatness should never be underestimated. Second, businesses should seek out and encourage the charismatic individuals within their ranks, much as Garcia's friends and bandmates sought him out and placed their trust in him.

Finally, every leader should cultivate his own charismatic qualities, and seek to inspire others in the same way Garcia inspired the Dead and their fans.

Know Your Limits

Charisma must be channeled in the proper direction so that it doesn't become simply an expression of ego. Garcia became noted for his humility, and he firmly rejected the role that many fans tried to force upon him—as a figurehead to a generation. At a time of profound social transformation, when all authority was being questioned, young people naturally looked around for new sources of wisdom. Some countercultural figures, such as Timothy Leary, were eager to don the mantle of guru, and this was precisely why the members of the Dead were suspicious of Leary. The Dead were radically democratic, and Garcia believed that anyone who accepted too much authority would become a demagogue. "I've made a real effort, so far anyway, to tell people that I'm not leading anybody anywhere," he once said, and he was especially sensitive to the dangers of large crowds, and of a group-think that could be exploited and pushed in a dangerous direction. "Would you like to have the responsibility of leading thousands of people off into some oblivion somewhere? If you thought that you were capable of it, you would automatically be the wrong person. So I'm disqualifying myself early." Maria Muldaur, who sang alongside Garcia, summed up his influence on his fans: "He had a flock. He didn't choose it. He didn't say 'I want to be a big icon and guru' to what is now several generations. But I think it was because in his own unassuming way he made himself completely an instrument of higher good energy."

Thinking of Garcia as an "instrument" makes sense, and not just because of the musical connotations. An instrument is a "means through which something is achieved," and Garcia fits the bill nicely. He was not an end in himself, but a means to a greater good—he inspired others to create great music, a strong community, and a better world. Northouse has written that a key quality of transformational leaders is "knowing their own strengths and weaknesses and emphasizing their strengths to [achieve] the overarching goals of the organization." Garcia always recognized his weaknesses, and always stayed focused on the larger good. He became an authority figure to several generations of Deadheads, but it was authority of the most benign sort: he was a wise uncle who, far from leading anyone astray, taught people to trust their hearts, count on their fellow humans, and be kind. Wary of his charisma, he channeled it in the one direction that made sense to him. He once said that he was interested in only one kind of power, and that was "the kind that frees people, not constrains them."

Inspire Greatness in Others

The most important ability of the transformational leader is providing inspiration and guidance to the entire organization. The goal, after all, is to transform the organization, to motivate everyone to relentlessly improve their performance. This was Garcia's key strength: he challenged people, both within his organization and in society at large, to achieve greatness, and many rose to the occasion.

For Garcia, as with all transformational leaders, the challenge to greatness started with himself. In his early years and throughout his career, he was anything but the aimless troubadour of legend. Instead, he drove himself to practice constantly because he wanted to be the best. "He was very ambitious. He wanted to do something big," according to Sara Garcia, his first wife. "The phrase that we used was 'destined for greatness.'" He knew, though, that fulfilling his destiny required a lot of hard work. "What I'm aware of now is his incredible single-minded drive," Sara said. "He would work on a single phrase for two days. Three days. Until he got it exactly right. I would love it when he got it right because he'd be pleased and happy for a moment and then he would go into the next one. He set high standards for himself and he would get in an absolute funk if he couldn't get something absolutely right."

That dedication to greatness inspired the rest of the band. Phil Lesh described Garcia as the Dead's "undeclared leader. As much as we all loved playing with one another, everyone's primary musical bond was with Jerry." Although aware of his leadership position, Garcia never became a prima donna onstage. "Although everyone adored Jerry's solos, the thing that made him such a magical player was how well he blended in and cooperated with the others," said Dead expert David Gans. "The glory of Jerry was that for many years he was almost never at a loss for a musical thought, but also never really obsessed with dominating everything."

Garcia's skill at knowing when to lead and when to follow carried over from the Dead's music into their business dealings. Take, for example, the way the band distributed royalties from its songs. In most bands this money goes strictly to the songwriters and lyricists. Garcia, though, described the written song as merely the "original creative flash" and shared royalties with every member of the band, who by performing helped create the finished version of the song. There could be no better metaphor for Garcia's way of doing business: he knew that he provided the spark of inspiration, but that the full expression of the Grateful Dead depended on contributions from all.

Jerry Garcia was a natural leader, and he expressed that leadership by denying it, thus leaving a space for others to perform at their best. The greatest leaders are not dictators, running organizations by decree. They have mastered the improvisational art of soloing at the head of the group, but also supporting—stepping into the background and letting others have their say.

Build a Culture of Transformation

Transformational leaders are so important to their organizations that they often raise concerns about succession: Will the company survive the loss of the leader? This was certainly true in the case of Garcia. In fact, what made his leadership skills all the more remarkable is that he was working under tremendous burdens. Like the breadwinner in a family whose finances are stretched thin, Garcia worried a lot about how to make ends meet. It wasn't a role he cherished, and he found refuge in drugs. In the late 1970s someone offered him a form of heroin that could be smoked. Garcia tried it, found that it smoothed out his pain, and was hooked. The drugs, combined with a sedentary lifestyle and a bad diet, contributed to serious health problems that included diabetes, lung problems, and heart disease. His efforts to get clean failed, as did the band's attempts to intervene. On August 9, 1995, while staying at a substance abuse clinic, Garcia died of a heart attack in his sleep. The nurse reported he had a smile on his face.

Garcia's importance to the band was never clearer

than after he departed. As Lesh said of Garcia's earlier absence due to illness, "Without Jerry's presence to pull us together, we were spinning further and further apart." In the months after his death, there were rumors that another guitarist—Carlos Santana, Eric Clapton, Jorma Kaukonen—would take over for him, but truly there was never much chance of a Grateful Dead without Jerry. In December 1995 the surviving band members announced that they had officially disbanded. Garcia was the sun that had held the band members in orbit; without him, they spun off into musical projects of their own.

Though the Grateful Dead as a band had ended, the Grateful Dead as a business organization, as a business model, and as a state of mind survives even today. The surviving members of the band continue to perform under names that have included the Dead, the Other Ones, Ratdog, Phil Lesh and Friends, and Furthur. The Deadheads survive, attending shows by these bands as well as by artists such as Phish, String Cheese Incident, Dark Star Orchestra, and the Dave Matthews Band. Those bands, in turn, follow the Grateful Dead's business model of relentless touring and strong customer service. Of course, the Grateful Dead as a business operation has remained profitable. Grateful Dead Productions has used its expertise to help other bands, handling tours and merchandising for acts including Bonnie Raitt and Alanis Morissette. The company has pushed beyond the world of music, taking on merchandising duties for the Oakland Raiders of the NFL, and has also released albums for the Allman Brothers Band and for David Crosby and Graham Nash. And, of course, Grateful Dead Productions has continued to sell trademarked Dead merchandise and Grateful Dead albums. One enormous success has been Dick's Picks, a series of live albums that captured the Dead's most important product: the stage performance before their adoring fans.

It's clear, then, that even without Jerry, the Dead have carried on.

How have they done it? Think of it in terms of another company run by a transformational leader: Southwest Airlines. In 1999, Herb Kelleher, Southwest's charismatic CEO, began treatment for prostate cancer, and analysts began speculating that the company would suffer in the absence of a leader so closely identified with its success. Kelleher, though, offered this reassurance: "The culture knows what to do." In other words, the transformational leader transforms the entire culture, providing it with a vision and a purpose, so that it can survive and thrive on its own. Garcia has lived on in his bandmates, Dead employees, and fans, all of whom know just what to do.

Build Trust

Garcia once told a funny story suggesting that his leadership was reluctant, or even accidental: "Here's something that used to happen all the time. The band would check in to a hotel. We'd get our room key and then we'd go to the elevator. Well, a lot of time we didn't have a clue where the elevator was. So what used to happen was that everybody would follow me, thinking that I would know. I'd be walking around thinking, why the . . . is everybody following me?"

Garcia categorized his form of leadership as a way of filling a vacuum. "If nobody else does it, I'll start something—it's a knack." What's important, though, is that Garcia was the one everyone chose to follow. No one blindly followed Kreutzmann or Weir or Hart. Whether Garcia liked it or not, he was the leader.

Asked in 1988 if he was the leader of the Grateful Dead, Garcia replied, "Not to any great extent, but the guys in the band all trust me." This emphasizes a key point: the band's functioning was built on trust. Business leadership theorists Bernard Bass and Bruce Avolio have argued that transformational leaders tend to be charismatic and hold their power based on the trust they inspire. This trust, in turn, inspires others in the organization to move beyond their self-interest for the good of the organization. Colleagues, in other words, are so inspired by their leader that they are driven to new heights of effort and creative output. These colleagues are "more capable of leading themselves, taking responsibility for their own actions, and gaining rewards through self-reinforcement."

Garcia certainly inspired such devotion. "When you played with Garcia, he could make you rise up to your full capacity," Peter Rowan said. "And I think it was reciprocal. He felt he could jump to his full capacity surrounded by the players he loved to play with. I never experienced any ego when he played." Garcia inspired such feelings not only in the musicians he played alongside but also in those who worked for the Dead's business organizations. "I had never been in it for the money. I was in it because of Jerry," said Richard Loren, a band manager. "I would have done anything for him because I loved him more than I love anything."

Garcia influenced his bandmates and his fans in a profound and positive way, changing their lives forever. He did what all true leaders do: he moved people. He moved them to travel thousands of miles, to live more principled lives. Garcia inspired the best in those with whom he worked and for whom he played. And they, in turn, inspired him to greater genius. It is this reciprocal effect—the willingness to learn while also teaching—that is Garcia's greatest lesson to the leaders of today. And, as we'll see in the next chapter, the members of the Grateful Dead organization took up the challenge and became leaders in their own right.

9

Share the Power

How the Dead Encouraged
Employees to Lead

Though Jerry Garcia was indisputably the leader of the Grateful Dead, he was not a dictator. Instead, he shared his power, helping to institute a flat organizational model in which all members of the Dead organization were treated well and helped make crucial decisions. One of the results: extremely satisfied employees. When Jerry Garcia was asked about the power held by even the lowliest band staff, he responded, "We're dragging them through life; shouldn't they have some say about it?"

Management theorists today call this practice "shared leadership." In their book on the topic, Craig Pearce and Jay Conger write that in this model, "leadership is broadly distributed among a set of individuals instead of centralized in the hands of a single individual who acts in the role of supervisor." The concept is closely allied with flat or horizontal management structures, which strip away multi-tier layers of management on the theory that workers are more productive when they have more direct control over work and the decisions surrounding it. Distributing power in this way leads to reduced stress for other leaders, better decision making, enhanced creativity, and more successful outcomes. Still, most organizations resist this approach, insisting that "core values must be pushed from the top down" and that a diffusion of leadership power would also lead to a loss of a sense of responsibility.

It's extremely difficult to establish a system of shared leadership, simply because rigid hierarchies are so deeply entrenched in our organizations and in our ways of thinking. But the Dead intuitively understood the importance of doing so. In their decision to give every employee—even the janitor—the power to veto decisions that affected the organization, they created a more flexible, responsive, and effective form of leadership. Band employees worked hard, remained creative, and stayed with the organization because they loved what they were doing and had a voice and a vested interest in the band's long-term success.

> **Grateful Dead Business Lesson 9:** Sharing leadership through horizontal organizational structures leads to better decision making and more loyal employees.

Think It Through

Bob Weir once recalled a time in the 1970s when promoter Bill Graham came to a band meeting and suggested that the band reorganize its business operation along more traditional lines. His ideas were roundly rejected. "Basically, he was too organized for us. We weren't ready for even that much structure. We were a complete democracy." The band never lost that commitment to democracy, but eventually they did feel the need to understand a bit better just how they were operating.

In 1981 they asked employee Alan Trist to create a report on band organization, an extraordinary document called "A Balanced Objective." It was surely the first time a rock 'n' roll band had devoted so much thought and effort to understanding how its organization worked. The document offers a revealing portrait of the values that underlay the Dead's operation.

The report, which runs to thirty-one double-spaced typed pages, opens with an introduction from Garcia, who strikes a serious note from the start. "This report shows how we really work," he writes. The band had incorporated as Grateful Dead Productions only "because the State of California requires that we identify ourselves as a business," and he insists that the corporation was "a legal fiction, not a working reality." The report was written, Garcia continues, "to free all the people in our organization from having to feel defined by what is actually an externally dictated fiction of convenience." Instead, the report would "distinguish the different kinds of work we do" and "appreciate the parts each of us plays."

Trist, the report's author, headed up the Dead's music publishing company. He also had studied anthropology at Cambridge University and functioned as what he called the band's "in-house social scientist." The report had been inspired, Trist writes in the introduction, by "disharmony in our relationships" that was caused by "ambiguity about responsibility for essential functions." The report doesn't reveal the precise nature of these frictions, but it's clear that the Dead's organizational model was causing problems precisely like those described by opponents of shared leadership theory: without a leader, division of responsibility can be unclear.

The Dead, though, weren't ready to throw in the towel. In his report, Trist insists upon the "broad range of creativity that we have among us and the need to combine these resources in flexible ways." And here we get to the heart of the matter, and the reason for the title "A Balanced Objective": "Our work situation then needs a balance between the structural requirements of taking care of its business and the fluid needs of its overall creative process." And this, really, is the balance that all organizations must strike— between the need for structure to get things done and the danger that such structure will stifle creativity.

The Dead, though, as masters of strategic improvisation, knew how to minimize structure while maximizing flexibility. As an example, Trist in the report takes a close look at the efforts that went into the band's various projects in 1980, the year that marked their fifteenth anniversary. There were two double live albums (*Reckoning* and *Dead Set*), the usual live concerts, a live video simulcast to fourteen theaters, a TV special for the Showtime cable network, a videodisc, and a special concert program illustrating the band's history. Trist carefully catalogs the enormous variety of work that went into organizing, promoting, and carrying out these highly successful projects. He emphasizes, though, that these efforts were carried out through not a hierarchical, command-and-control business model, but an ad hoc method that called on every employee's highest talents. "To define the 'flexible group process' is to lose it," he writes. "Its value lies in the spontaneity which comes from acknowledgement of it and openness to the unknown next point of invention."

The language can be a little vague, but that's by design. Best utilization of talent required flexibility, so that everyone could apply his or her skills in the manner that could best contribute to each particular project. "A Balanced Objective" shows that sharing leadership wasn't easy, but that it offered considerable benefits. The Dead were willing to work at it to reap the rewards.

Choose Employees Carefully

Selecting the right employees is key to attempting shared leadership. Charles Koch, CEO of Koch Industries, has this to say in *The Science of Success*: "Rogue employees who operate out of personal interest are minimized by selecting and retaining employees foremost on values and belief." The Grateful Dead, though a world away from Koch in most political and cultural matters, would have agreed with him completely on this point. As Dennis McNally put it, "Dead employee qualifications started with loyalty, honesty, and compatibility." Specific skills could be evaluated later; first, the band had to know you would fit in.

After the band had gone through a rough patch, Garcia asked David Parker, a fellow musician and old friend, to help manage them. "The main interest at the time for Jerry and the rest of the band was in finding someone they felt they could trust to handle their money," Parker said. He had some business experience, but just as important, he was a known quantity. Steve Brown, who worked for Grateful Dead Records, recalled his first meeting with Jerry Garcia, whom he worshipped and desperately wanted to work for. "This was my shot. I went in there and I had everything I needed to know about the record business just nailed to the tits. Everything he could ask me, I knew I could answer it." So what happened? "He

didn't ask me one thing about the record business."
Instead, "We talked about growing up in San Francisco.
We talked about what kind of music experiences we'd
both had. We talked about the kind of art we liked. We
talked about all kinds of music. We laughed a lot, told
some funny stories, and barely got into any kind of talk
at all about record business stuff. He was checking me
out and hanging with me. It was a thing really of vibing
out if he could work with me out of the blue."

That "vibing out" process was crucial. Zappos, the
online retailer, is one major company that has adopted
a similar process, attempting to create an environment
so meaningful and so enjoyable that people will want to
hang out there even if they aren't getting paid. For this
to be true, workers generally have to enjoy one another's company, so managers focus on compatibility and
shared values when conducting interviews and making
decisions. The same was true within the Grateful Dead.
Given the dispersed leadership structure of the band's
organization, it was important that they have a shared
vision of how their business should operate.

Pay Generously

With so much responsibility placed on their shoulders,
the Dead's road crew demanded to be treated well, and
they were. Companies have long known that treating

employees well is good for the bottom line, but they often don't put those principles into practice. It tends to be firms in the most competitive industries—these days, software and Internet companies—that offer the best benefits as a way to retain the most talented employees. The Grateful Dead came to the same conclusion, but for different reasons. They didn't offer good benefits and high pay out of concern that employees might jump ship and go work for the Rolling Stones. Instead, the Dead's employee culture emerged as a matter of principle: everyone who worked for the band was considered a member of the family, so they deserved to have their voices heard and to be well compensated for their labor.

During the period in the mid-sixties when the band lived at 710 Ashbury, musicians and employees all made the same amount: everybody, from office workers and roadies right on up to Garcia, made twenty-five dollars a week. By the early 1970s, when the band started doing better, the employees shared the wealth. Richard Loren, a manager during this period, said the Dead were "paying their employees far more than the going rate." Dennis McNally, who joined the crew as biographer/publicist in 1984, said that at that time there were standard salaries, according to three major divisions: office worker, crew, and engineer. He started off making the lowest salary for office workers, which was $26,000, though bonuses generally brought that up to $35,000 or so. Crew members would complain that office workers, who got to sleep at home in their own beds, got the same bonuses as the crew, who had to hump equipment from city to city. Garcia explained the philosophy: "We don't give out bonuses for the amount of work you do. It's because we have extra money."

In addition to generous salary and bonuses, other policies were employee-friendly. Minutes of a band meeting in 1984 reveal that when bookkeeper Janet Soto-Knudsen was having a baby, the board approved "maternity leave...at full salary and for whatever time she needs." After the Dead single "Touch of Grey" soared to number nine on the charts in 1987, the band entered an entirely new realm in earning, and they shared the wealth. When McNally asked for a raise, they doubled his salary. "The nineties were good," he commented.

A number of employees earned more than $100,000 a year, and all enjoyed benefits that included a pension fund, health insurance, educational funds for their children, and a profit-sharing arrangement that involved not only tour revenues but also song royalties. Oh, and yes, during these flushest of flush years, the crew members had their own Learjet. Okay, so the jet was a little over the top, but the message is clear: the Dead did well by their employees. And remember that the band was generous by any standards, but particularly by those of the music industry, where generally bands hired crews only for the length of the tour. McNally, in his band biography, goes so far as to say, "The crew had better pay, better working

conditions, and more influence on the band's decisions...
than any employees of any music group ever."

Why did they do it? Partly for reasons of philosophy:
they wanted to shake up the business world, and they
believed in treating people in a human way rather than
as cogs in a machine. And partly because it was practical: the Dead spent so much time on the road, and relied
so heavily on their crews, that they needed professional,
full-time employees who knew the band inside out to
make sure the entire operation ran smoothly.

That treatment paid off. For instance, in 1994, their
top-grossing year, the Dead had seventy employees and
no turnover at all. Absenteeism was almost nil. Ram
Rod, the crew chief, with his twenty-eight years of ten-
ure when the band broke up, offered merely the most
extreme example of employee loyalty. When the Dead
hired you, you stayed hired, and you stayed happy. It is
a lesson that's finally hitting home for many companies
today. Tony Hsieh, celebrated CEO of Zappos, argues
that it's "actually possible to run a values-based business
that also focuses on everyone's happiness." The Dead
proved that lesson many years ago.

Build Consensus

By the late 1980s the Dead had become a large organization, grossing in the tens of millions of dollars annually.

The official board of directors met mostly at band meetings, but once a month there was also an all-employee meeting. Everyone was present at these meetings, Alan Trist recalled, from "the lowliest cook and bottle washer, as it were, to all the band members, twenty or thirty people in the room at the same time." And everyone's opinion carried weight—any major decision required consensus, from every last person at the meeting.

The album *American Beauty* was originally supposed to feature a photo on the back cover in which some members were holding guns, but Robert Hunter protested that "these were incendiary and revolutionary times, and I did not want this band to be making that statement." And because one "no" was a veto, they went with a different photo. "The bottom line was that if one guy didn't want to do something, they wouldn't do it. That was the Dead principle," said producer Peter Barsotti. Someone could propose "this huge beautiful plan. One guy saying, 'I don't wanna,' and that was the end of it. You'd resent it and really feel frustrated. But if you thought about it, that was the reason they could exist. That was the only way they could possibly go on as a group." Hal Kant, the band's longtime lawyer, explained the benefits of this sometimes frustrating process. "The insanity of those meetings had a certain beneficial effect, because you heard every point of view," he said. "I don't remember a vote—if they can't turn around a dissenter, they don't do it—and therefore, when they do something, they have everybody behind it. It means they don't do anything reluctantly." This is one of the key benefits of shared leadership: if everyone has a say in the decision, then you get complete buy-in from the staff. And with complete buy-in comes superior performance.

McNally recalled a time when Bill Graham visited a board meeting and made a suggestion. Willy Legate, though, dismissed it as "commercial." The idea was finished. Legate was the building superintendent for the Dead. Bill Graham, millionaire and hotshot executive, had been shot down by a janitor. Weir later explained that the structure of the organization must "take into account everybody's contributions. Not just the musicians' or the management's but the people who do the grunt work as well. Everybody. Everybody has to contribute as a team, and however you set up your business mechanisms, they should reflect everybody's efforts and contributions. If they do, chances are the organization is not going to fold on itself and be diseased from within."

The most celebrated instance of the Dead's egalitarian spirit came in 1971, in a meeting with their record label. Having recently released *Workingman's Dead* and *American Beauty* with Warner Bros., the Dead had two commercially successful studio albums under their belt. Now they were putting the finishing touches on a live album. During one of the regular all-employee meetings, Lesh suggested that the album be titled *Skullfuck*. He didn't especially like Warner Bros., and suggested the name in part to tweak them, but the idea quickly took hold among all the others at the meeting. What better way to show the world that success hadn't changed them? It was unanimous: the album would be called *Skullfuck*. The Dead had artistic control over the album, which included the title. Manager Jon McIntire called Joe Smith at Warner Bros. and told him of the choice of names. "You can't do this to me!" Smith shouted. McIntire responded, "It's not *me*, Joe. It's *all* of us. We're *all* doing this to you." Which shows what Smith was up against: he didn't have to convince one person that *Skullfuck* was an unwise choice of names; he had to convince the entire organization, so he asked for a meeting. "But any decision that concerned them had to involve everybody in the band," Smith said, "and their *families* were involved in the decision as well, and the other people associated with them...so it was necessary to hold a meeting with all of them."

As a result, fifty-five members of the Dead organization boarded a plane and flew from San Francisco to Los Angeles. The Warner Bros. conference room wouldn't hold them, so Smith rented a conference room at the Continental Hyatt. Spencer Dryden, drummer for New Riders of the Purple Sage, recalled the meeting: "Everyone in the room took a turn in trying to explain to these straight guys from Warners why it made perfect sense for the record to be called *Skullfuck*. People had these long explanations, explaining the word on all sorts of different levels, totally serious." Joe Smith, though, played it like a pro, convincing the band that the bad guy wasn't him but the buyers for department stores. He asked, "Do you want to sell ten thousand copies?" The fifty-five members of the Dead entourage ultimately agreed to a change. Instead of *Skullfuck*, the album was self-titled, and it's considered one of their best. To ease the pain of giving up their preferred title, the Dead got a generous promotional budget for the album, including $100,000 for broadcasting concerts on the radio. The promotions, coupled with the quality of the record, worked: the album sold far, far more than ten thousand copies; it was their first album to go gold.

Garcia later suggested that the episode was a bit of a prank. "We had a big meeting with Warners. They were horrified! They were shocked! . . . so we finally backed down, but it was more of a joke on our part." In the end, the Dead had it both ways. They agreed, as a team, to insist on *Skullfuck*; they had a delightful time, as a team, flying to Los Angeles to meet with the terrified people at Warner Bros.; and they decided, as a team, to withdraw their demand for the troublesome title. In the end, they had it their way: they had a grand adventure, tweaked Warner Bros., and still got a gold record out of the deal.

What emerges from this story is another benefit of shared leadership: the sense of camaraderie, of common enterprise, that it produces. Traditional leadership structures sometimes produce an us-versus-them mentality, in which labor is pitted against management. In shared leadership, the "us" is the entire company, and the "them" is the outside world that attempts to thwart them. By spreading authority broadly throughout the organization, the Dead created a fierce sense of loyalty, from Garcia all the way down to the janitor. And that means that everyone gave his all to the organization.

Share Responsibility

Because of the band's commitment to shared leadership, the crew took on a great deal of authority—not only traditional roadie duties but executive positions as well.

A few key members of the crew shouldered the heaviest burden. The former Merry Prankster Larry Shurtliff, known as Ram Rod, became the Dead's equipment manager in 1967 and never left. Raised in Oregon's ranch country, he was recognized as not only reliable and competent but also unassuming and honest, the ethical compass of the band. Next in seniority to Ram Rod was Steve Parish, who met Ram Rod while ushering in New York City in 1969. Six foot five and 250 pounds, Parish was large and loud and exactly the man they needed to impose a minimum amount of order on the chaos of the tour. Along with the heavy lifting, Parish also had a delicate daily task: changing the strings on Garcia's and

Weir's guitars. He would eventually become Garcia's personal manager.

This is how tight and loyal the crew was: when drummer Mickey Hart fired Steve Parish, Ram Rod swapped jobs with him, taking the post with the demanding Hart and letting Parish become Garcia's guitar roadie so he would still have a job. Working for Garcia was a better job, but Ram Rod gave it up to keep the team together, because he knew that having Parish on board was good for the operation. Not a shy man, Parish was aware of his, and the crew's, value. "We're part of the Dead," he said. "You really put your whole heart into the system."

According to Alan Trist, at one point some people connected to the band suggested that they should "structure the Grateful Dead along more traditional lines," to outsource the management and to hire crew members only when they were needed on the road, rather than keep them on salary year round. The suggestion didn't go over well. "I remember Weir laughing. It cracked him up," Trist said. "He said, 'You mean somebody who doesn't know how to plug in my amp is going to do it for me?'" The idea died there.

But this road crew did far more than plug in amps. In what is perhaps the most surprising instance of shared leadership, crew member Ram Rod not only handled the drums but also became a member of the Dead's board of directors and president of the band's corporation,

Grateful Dead Productions Inc. This reflected Ram
Rod's competence and the band's trust in him, and also
provided a big boost to the crew: seeing one of their own
entrusted with so much authority taught them that the
Grateful Dead truly was an egalitarian organization,
where everyone's talents were recognized and their opinions valued. And Ram Rod wasn't the only one. Parish
became manager of one of Garcia's solo projects. Lesh's
bass roadie, Bill "Kidd" Candelario, became the head of
Grateful Dead Merchandising.

And it wasn't just about skilled roadies. "Most job
descriptions are narrow, and what we're looking to do is
expand, rather than narrow," Garcia explained. "Rather
than thinking of your job being *this*, let's open it out to
this. Why do you only want to define yourself as a person who does only this, this, and this? You know what
I mean? And why should your job be less than you are?
If your contribution can be greater, then what we'll do is
invent a reason for it to be greater. Dig?" Most corporations don't "dig," but they should. The Dead actually put
to work the ideas embodied in their "Balanced Objective" report. They minimized structure, downplayed
job descriptions, and asked everyone to pitch in however
they could best contribute. The Dead's success speaks for
itself. Other companies, by chopping back their thickets
of hierarchy, could experience similar success. As Mickey
Hart said, "Nobody is anybody's boss."

Share the Wealth, Share the Power

"What made the Dead so great was their willingness to cooperate," Garcia biographer Blair Jackson wrote. "Although everyone adored Jerry's solos, the thing that made him such a magical player was how well he blended in and cooperated with the others." Though referring explicitly to music, this isn't a bad way to describe employee empowerment. Both management and employees must alternate between following and leading, in order to deal with unexpected situations. By sharing leadership, and flattening the organizational chart, the Dead opened themselves up to success.

Recent studies of shared leadership have found that it flourishes in an environment that nurtures a sense of shared purpose, social support, and employee voice. This perfectly describes the atmosphere the Dead fostered. "Wisdom is where you find it," Garcia once said. "Every point of view at its very worst will see something that you don't see." That, in a nutshell, is the guiding spirit of decision making within the Grateful Dead organization.

It should also be the guiding spirit of every organization. When you listen to every voice, everyone is empowered, and everyone takes responsibility for his or her own actions. When employees have power in the process and a stake in the outcome, they are much more committed and successful. When people know that their ideas count, they grow more loyal to the organization, work harder, and contribute better, more creative ideas.

Best of all, it works. "It doesn't work like General Motors does, but it works," Garcia said. "And it's more fun."

10

Exploit the Experience Economy

How the Dead Kept It Real

People today "see the world in terms of real and fake, and want to buy something real from someone genuine, and not a fake from some phony," according to James H. Gilmore and B. Joseph Pine II in their book *Authenticity: What Consumers Really Want.* In a world where "reality TV" isn't real, and where online personas have thrown true identity into question, people have a hunger for the genuine. Bombarded by the false, they seek the real.

The new focus for businesses, Gilmore and Pine say, must be on "rendering authenticity"—a phrase they say "should one day roll trippingly off the tongue as easily as 'controlling costs' and 'improving quality.'" We are undergoing a shift from a service economy toward an "experience economy," in which we pay money for activities that make us feel we are finding our true selves. Starbucks can set its coffee drink prices so high because what it's really selling is the experience of store ambience and a skilled barista. Whereas quality-minded consumers focus on how well a product is made, the authenticity-minded consumers purchase "on the basis of conforming to self-image." In the new experience economy, we buy the products and services that make us most truly ourselves.

But there's a dilemma at the center of this quest for authenticity: If you're trying too hard to create authentic experiences, doesn't that turn you into a fake? The Grateful Dead offer a way out of this dilemma. Garcia and friends, after all, might be considered the poster boys of authenticity, in their music and their lives. "For me, it's always emotional—can I live with this song? I'm going to have to get onstage and be this song," Garcia said. "I'm going to have to represent this point of view, this idea. And if it doesn't work for me, I can't do it. I can't act, you know? So there has to be something authentic about it." What was true of Garcia in his singing was true of everything the band did: they couldn't act; they could only be genuine. And they were most truly themselves performing live in front of an audience. Pioneers of the experience economy, the Dead remained genuine by staying true to their core values and their heritage, and by providing a transcendent musical experience for their fans.

> **Grateful Dead Business Lesson 10:** Provide your customers with authentic experiences that improve their lives.

Keep Your Passion for the Product

Customers know when a business is operating for the wrong reasons. When the frozen dessert company Pinkberry became a sensation, a host of imitators popped up, many offering products and storefront styles to rival the original. But customers were suspicious, because they recognized that these imitators were simply riding the coattails of the true innovator, trying to make a buck on someone else's idea. The same is true in music. Why is it that "boy bands" appeal only to the youngest fans and have such short shelf lives? Because true music fans know that the bands are phony, a collection of singers put together to match a marketing formula, interested in earning money rather than advancing the art of popular music. Real fans know that this type of music comes from a place of greed, not passion.

There was never any doubt about the passion of the Grateful Dead. Jerry Garcia, for starters, got his first guitar at age fifteen and was rarely spotted without one for the rest of his life. Learning to play rock guitar was "a revelation...the key to heaven," Garcia once said. In the early 1960s, when he fell in with the tail end of the Beat crowd in Palo Alto, friends report that he was never not practicing. "That's *all* he did," one said. "He played music. He was totally dedicated." That passion never died, not for Jerry and not for the rest of the band. Read through David Gans's wonderful book of interviews, *Conversations with the Dead*, for instance, or the oral biography *Dark Star*, or the band members' own memoirs, and you'll be struck by how they never lost their enthusiasm for what they did. You'll run across Garcia' saying things like this, from 1981: "I have an interesting treatise by this Dutch guy about medieval church music." When you hear Lesh expounding on the history of electronic music, or Hart on non-Western time signatures and Tibetan chanting, or Bob Weir on learning to play slide guitar—you know these are people who loved to play and who never stopped.

All of them were, or became, talented musicians. But they weren't virtuosos, and they didn't get by on chops. They got by on love and determination. "It's not as though we're especially gifted," Garcia said, "but we have been exceptionally determined." Later, he explained the lesson he drew from the band's career. "If you're able to enjoy something, to devote your life to it...it will work out for you. It will work," he said. "We [The Grateful Dead] agreed to stick it out past what would normally have been discouraging experiences." And they stuck it out because they had an authentic passion for their work and for sharing that experience with others.

John Dawson, who later played with Garcia in New Riders of the Purple Sage, described Garcia's playing as an addiction, not unlike the heroin habit he later developed. "He was a picking junkie," Dawson said. "Before he got to be uncomfortable without some heroin in his blood, he got to be uncomfortable without a guitar in his hand. That was his first draw." The addiction comparison might be overstated, but it does give a sense of the passion and commitment required for success. There are plenty of teenagers who acquire guitars, but not many devote themselves to the project with the passion that Garcia did.

Given that rock 'n' roll was in its youth in the 1950s, the best comparison might be to the first generation of computer pioneers. The young Steve Jobs and the young Bill Gates acquired not cheap guitars but crude computers, and they worked with them ceaselessly to create something new. They all had talent, sure, but without that passion we're unlikely ever to have heard of any of them. That passion created great products, to be sure, but it also translated into an unmistakable quality of authenticity. Customers who buy an Apple computer or an album from the Dead know they are getting the real deal: a material expression of a passionate commitment to innovation and excellence.

Stay True to Your Roots

Most authentic brands have a long heritage: Levi's, Coca-Cola (despite its New Coke misstep), Harley-Davidson, L.L.Bean. While moving into the future, they honor the past. According to Gilmore and Pine, authentic businesses always remember where and when they originated, because these origins shaped the identity of the company. Many brands now celebrate this essence, often called "corporate DNA," through interactive museums, such as World of Coca-Cola in Atlanta or Major League Baseball's Hall of Fame in Cooperstown, New York. By honoring the past, companies remind their customers of the brand's deep meaning, and the experience of consumption becomes that much richer.

In the rock 'n' roll business, staying true to your roots is a tricky proposition. Bands practice for years, struggling to pay the rent, playing crummy venues, and living out of vans. And then as soon as they gain a measure of success—sign with a label, play larger venues, sell merchandise—they are accused of selling out. This issue was especially problematic for the Grateful Dead, whose origins lay in the anticorporate sixties counterculture. It was, in many ways, a no-win situation—but the Dead found a way to win, remaining authentic while achieving mainstream success.

From the start, the band focused on making music,

rejecting the drive for rapid growth and the accumulation of wealth. As Lesh explained, "Although we had to be a 'business' in order to survive and continue to make music together, we were not buying into the traditional pop music culture of fame and fortune." Garcia put it even more simply: "We never said that money was bad, but it has just never been our focus one way or the other, pro or con," Garcia said. The vision of the Grateful Dead was to play music; the business plan was designed not to make them rich but to allow them to make enough money to do that. By focusing on their art, not their finances, the band helped ensure that its image would remain authentic.

People tend to recall the Dead from their years of mega-success after 1987, but for the first two decades of their career they were a working band, making a living but not a fortune. For their earliest gigs in the Bay Area, they were paid $125. Their communal house at 710 Ashbury Street operated on pooled finances, with everyone drawing a small allowance. By the late sixties they could pull in a few thousand dollars for a good show, but it still wasn't covering expenses. By the early seventies, they were making truly good money, in the tens of thousands for a large stadium show or a festival. Alan Trist summarized the band's mission to stay true to its roots. "In the early seventies, the band was growing up and becoming a bigger deal," but even then "the desire was to have people who were cool and part of that family scene." The band was pushed toward business practices that didn't conform to its values, but it resisted, insisting on hiring people who "were both friends and business associates to take care of what needed to be taken care of and interface with the outside world," making sure the band's values and vision were upheld.

Any band can remain authentic as long as it remains poor. The true test is what happens when the money starts flowing. And the Dead passed this test. When the income started flowing, the band members didn't keep it all for themselves. Instead, they invested it in what they cared about: people, music, good causes. As we've seen, they paid generous wages and benefits to staff members, spent enormous sums on sound systems to improve the fan experience, and donated their time and their cash to a wide range of charitable causes. All of these actions demonstrated to the fans that vast wealth hadn't changed the band's values—the money just allowed the Dead to carry their musical mission even further.

The Dead were rooted in the culture of the sixties, and they always honored that heritage. Even more important, they honored their *musical* heritage. As musical styles came and went, the Dead stuck to their starkly original brand of improvisational music. "The public's taste runs in cycles," Phil Lesh said, "and what's trendy twenty years ago is not the same thing that's going to be trendy today. But while the public's tastes go up and down in cycles, we're just like the median line that's running right through that." That in itself is a good definition of authenticity: a straight line running through the rising and falling waves of fad. Fans seeking authentic experiences—whether a bottle of soda or a baseball game—don't chase trends; they seek out the brands that transcend trends.

Be Transparent

At its most basic level, authenticity means presenting one's true face to the world. And that involves being open with the customer about everything regarding your business—your plans, your successes, your failures. Remember Starbucks's troubles from a few years back, when it expanded too fast, lost touch with its roots, and became a simulacrum of its old self, patently inauthentic to its formerly loyal customers? Sales were off, the company was in trouble, and what did the executives do? They admitted their mistakes, apologized for having strayed from their roots, and asked their customers for suggestions as to how to get back on the right track. Now people may remember the problems, but they also remember the graceful and open way the company recovered.

Transparency prevailed both within the organization and in its relations with customers. As we've seen, the Dead maintained a flat organizational structure throughout their career, and shared leadership with every employee.

The organization held regular all-employee meetings, and any "no" vote, even from the lowliest of employees, was enough to scuttle a project. The Dead had nothing to hide, so there was no reason for a bunker mentality.

This same transparency applied to the Dead's dealings with their fans. The newsletter the band started mailing out in the early 1970s was remarkably frank, detailing the economics of the band's operation and the problems it encountered along the way. What's more, the Dead invited communications from the fans, and actually paid attention to the feedback they received, using it to affect everything from playlists to venues to which live recordings to release. The most important point of contact, however, occurred on the road. Starbucks management failed by temporarily falling out of touch with their customers. That's something that never happened to the Grateful Dead. Because they toured so much, they never lost the transparency brought on by proximity.

Provide Authentic Experiences

In the new "experience economy," Gilmore and Pine argue, people are looking for the authentic experience, "memorable events that engage them in an intensely personal way." The key to the Dead's success lay precisely in creating such events. You might say that engaging people in such intense ways was at the core of their mission. This mission had its origins in the sixties psychedelic scene, because LSD was nothing if not an intense experience, what Garcia described as "a series of continually opening doors," a way to deeper knowledge of self and community. The Acid Tests and the Human Be-In were extensions of this quest for a deeper human experience, and the Dead extended this model to their entire touring life.

You need not look far for evidence that fans became Deadheads because of the deep experiences being a Dead fan offered. "What we're about is not entertainment or advertising," Lesh once said. "Mickey used to say we're in the transportation business—we move minds." Joseph Campbell, the great scholar of mythology, became enthralled by the Dead after seeing a show in 1985—the first rock concert he attended. "This is Dionysus talking through these kids," he said afterward. "Now I've seen similar manifestations, but nothing as innocent as what I saw with this bunch. This was sheer innocence. And when the great beam of light would go over the crowd, you'd see these marvelous young faces in sheer rapture—for five hours! Packed together like sardines! Eight thousand of them! . . . This is a wonderful, fervent loss of self in the larger self of homogeneous community. This is what it's all about."

People turned to the Dead for an experience that would stay with them and transform their lives. "For me it was the only experience that would make me feel good and cleansed and alive and regenerated," said Thayer Craw, a longtime friend of the band. "No matter what was happening in the world or in your life, you went to a show and it made you feel wonderful and you could actually sustain that feeling for a long time."

This was the peak experience that the Dead offered, concert after concert, seventy or eighty nights a year. Ned Lagin, a musician who toured with the Dead in the 1970s, said the Dead offered people the opportunity to transform themselves: "I think the importance of the Grateful Dead is simply this: it's rediscovering the mythical possibilities... of everyday life, in terms of fulfillment, in terms of following your own dreams, in terms of being who you want to be." The most successful companies in the experience economy will help people do exactly that.

Don't Try Too Hard

For the Grateful Dead, the issue of authenticity never really came up; it was just assumed. Their business arose from a deep-seated passion for making music; the businesses they organized and the money they made were simply a means to follow their passions. You can't get any more authentic than that, which is why the Dead were at the forefront of the new experience economy.

The Dead's values—to make the world a better, more humane place—animated everything they did, and their fans recognized that. The investment in sound systems, in higher-quality records, and in top-notch customer service were all evidence that they truly cared about their fans. Consideration like that can't be faked. The truth lay in the experience of being a Grateful Dead fan, of going to shows and interacting with the band and with other fans. Deadheads responded to this experience by staying fans, and by recruiting new fans to the tribe. In an authentic relationship, customers won't be put off by a few mistakes or stolen away by a lower-priced offering. An authentic relationship arises because your business satisfies a deep need within someone, making him think—*know*, because it's true and not just an illusion— that he can be more fully himself in relationship with your products or services.

The online world creates challenges and opportunities in the realm of authenticity. It's easier than ever to create an ersatz authenticity, an illusion of heritage, of community, of caring, when none exists. But the Web also offers the tools for customers to share information with one another, to ferret out the real from the fake. And if you're real, your customers will thank you and help you by spreading the news on Twitter and Facebook, Amazon and Yelp. The Grateful Dead's advice to business owners would read something like this: If you don't care about what you're doing, with all your heart and all your soul, don't do it. Bob Weir offered some advice to young musicians, and the same would apply to any businessperson:

"Make sure you're entirely engrossed in it," Weir said. "If you're not enjoying it…it's going to get old, and it'll sound like it." Customers, like music fans, can spot a phony. Don't just act authentic; be authentic. Be who you are, and do what you do passionately. Your customers will recognize the real thing when they see it.

Epilogue

The Accidental Capitalists

The Dead show that changed my life took place on June 14, 1985, at the Greek Theatre in Berkeley. At that time I had been to seven previous shows, become a taper, and collected bootleg tapes and LPs. This show was part of a run celebrating the band's twentieth anniversary, and I was lucky to get in—I didn't yet know about Grateful Dead Ticket Sales but had managed to stay on the phone with Ticketmaster long enough to score.

The show was a remarkable thing to behold. Although I was fifteen hundred miles from home, everyone in the crowd seemed like an old friend. Just before the band came out, the PA began to play the Beatles' "Sgt. Pepper": "It was twenty years ago today, Sgt. Pepper taught the band to play..." And then out came the Dead. They began to play "Dancin' in the Streets," and the whole place took off. The entire audience was up and dancing, and they kept it up for the entire show. For the first time, I really started dancing, too, and I haven't stopped dancing since. The connections were so clear as I danced: I was connected to other fans, the fans were connected to the band, and we were all connected to the music. As I watched the crowd move and listened to the music, I knew this experience was something magical that held important lessons—for business and for life. The Dead were a collaborative team who knew how to listen to one another, take turns, and share. They reached out to their customers and helped them create a community, involving them in a remarkable human experience. They strove constantly, regardless of expense, to create the greatest possible musical experience. I knew then that I had to tell this story.

I remember my first encounter with the Grateful Dead organization, back in 1974, when I owned and operated Barry's Record Rack in Kansas City. My store was small and not part of a chain, so most record companies ignored it. But one day the Dead's sales rep appeared in the shop and gave me his card, a T-shirt advertising two new releases (I still have it), and posters for my store (including one for *Grateful Dead from the Mars Hotel*). This was during the period when the band was trying to get Grateful Dead Records up and running, so their reps were making an extra effort to reach out to independent shops like mine, the ones that could add a personal touch to the marketing of records. The rep did his job well, because his pitch was so deeply felt. He took me to lunch and shared stories of how much the Dead meant to him, including how the band had supported him when he had been incarcerated. It was about the music, but it was also about more than that—it was about loyalty, kindness, and community.

As it happened, those values also led the way to vast profits. "If there's such a thing as a recession-proof band, the Grateful Dead must be it," a journalist wrote amid a recession in 1991. "While the rest of the music industry has suffered through one of its worst years ever—record sales have plummeted, and the bottom has virtually fallen out of the concert business—the Dead have trouped along, oblivious as ever to any trends, either economical or musical." The Dead were recession-proof precisely because they stayed true to themselves, avoided trends, and remained focused on fundamentals. Most surprisingly, they had a firmer grasp of those fundamentals than almost anyone in the record industry or American business in general.

Rather than focusing on the needs of shareholders (in the Dead's case, the band members), they paid more attention to the needs of customers—with information hotlines, priority access to tickets, personal attention to complaints, stellar sound systems, and low ticket prices.

Rather than outsourcing key functions—such as record production, merchandising, and ticket sales—the Dead insourced them to ensure the highest quality products and service.

Rather than cutting back on staffing costs—by relying on temporary crew, as was standard in the industry—the Dead kept workers on full time, year round, to ensure skilled support services for the band and its fans.

Rather than insisting on the rigid hierarchical structures standard in the business world, the Dead instituted a shared leadership structure in which any member of the organization, even a janitor, could veto any proposal.

Rather than demanding a rigid separation of business and customer, producer and consumer, the Dead insisted that their enterprise be a collaboration between the band and its fans.

When the default position of most companies was to attack trademark and copyright infringers indiscriminately, the Dead adopted a nuanced position, suing profit-oriented bootleggers but permitting noncommercial (or minimally commercial) use by fans. In doing so, they became pioneers in the concept of "free," giving away content and making money in other ways. They grasped the business model of the Internet before it even existed.

That's quite a legacy of innovation, and the Dead were so far ahead of the curve precisely because they rejected the standard ways of doing things. Their desire to improvise a new business model led to a large number of miscues, but it produced even more moments of inspiration and innovation. As in improvised music, bum notes and bad performances were the price paid for eruptions of genius. In describing some of his early musical adventures, Jerry Garcia once said, "I was out on a limb like a motherfucker." The same could be said for the band as a whole, in their personal lives, their music, and their business dealings. When you spend most of your time out on a limb, there's a good chance you'll crash to the ground now and then, but you'll also have a much better view of the future.

The Dead's business innovation sprang in part from a deep commitment to values. They insisted on innovating the highest quality sound systems because they had an ethic that the ticket buyer in the last row deserved to hear the concert as well as the ticket buyer in the front row. They started their own record company because they were embarrassed that their fans had been forced to buy low-quality recordings put out by Warner Bros. They provided stellar customer service because, as Garcia put it, Deadheads were "nice people" and deserved to be treated well. They shared leadership with employees because it was the right thing to do. They allowed taping because they trusted their fans to follow the rules, sharing the recordings but not selling them. They played free shows, created a foundation, and donated money because they wanted to live in a better world. Indeed, nearly all of their actions were committed to that goal of social transformation—proving that the world could be run in a more humane way.

Pete Townshend, guitarist for the Who, a very different style of rock band, admired the Grateful Dead's attitude toward life and business. "They enjoyed one another's company," Townshend said. "One of them might walk off halfway through and go chat with somebody. It was slow. It was easy. They were taking their time. They were being almost mystical about the process. They were not striving for success. There was no stress."

They were not striving for success, and yet they achieved success. Or, perhaps, they achieved success *because* they were not striving for it. Too many businesses today keep their eyes focused squarely on the bottom line and are shocked when profits elude them. Or they are shocked when profits arrive suddenly, then disappear just as quickly when their employees and customers move on to the next big thing. The Dead kept their focus on their vision and their values. Success flowed from there.

"All decisions were made based on the integrity of the music," publicist and historian Dennis McNally said. "Many simply turned out to be great business decisions as well."

Those looking to make great business decisions would do well to follow their lead.

List of Key Sources

60 Minutes II: Transcript, "Reviving the Dead: The Surviving Members of the Grateful Dead Tour Again as the Dead," hosted by Charlie Rose, November 12, 2003.

Rebecca Adams, "A Community of Friends," draft manuscript, provided courtesy of author.

Rebecca G. Adams and Robert Sardiello, eds., *Deadhead Social Science* (Walnut Creek, Calif.: AltaMira Press, 2000).

Chris Anderson, *Free: The Future of a Radical Price* (New York: Hyperion, 2009).

John Perry Barlow, "The Economy of Ideas: A Framework for Patents and Copyrights in the Digital Age," *Wired*, March 1994, www.wired.com/wired/archive/2.03/economy.ideas_pr.html.

Barry Barnes, "Strategic Improvisation: Management Lessons from the Dead," in *The Grateful Dead in Concert: Essays on Live Improvisation*, ed. Jim Tuedio and Stan Spector (Jefferson, N.C.: McFarland Publishing, 2010).

Barry Barnes, "The Grateful Dead—Creating Deadheads by Providing Drop Dead Customer Service," in *Superior Customer Value in the New Economy: Concepts, Cases and Applications*, W. C. Johnson and A. Weinstein (Boca Raton, FL: St. Lucie Press, 2004).

Barry Barnes, "A Conversation with Dan Healy," *Unbroken Chain* 6, no. 3 (1991).

Barry Barnes interview with David Gans, October 17, 1998.

Barry Barnes interview with Peter McQuaid, October 13, 1998.

Barry Barnes interview with Dennis McNally, July 2000.

Barry Barnes interview with David Parker, March 2000.

Barry Barnes interview with Alan Trist, June 30, 2010.

F. J. Barrett, "Creativity and Improvisation in Jazz and Organizations: Implications for Organizational Learning," *Organizational Science* 9 (1998): 605–22.

B. M. Bass and B. J. Avolio, "The Implications of Transactional and Transformational Leadership for Individual, Team, and Organizational Development," *Research in Organizational Change and Development* 4 (1990): 231–72.

Alexander Bloom and Wini Breines, *"Takin' It To the Streets": A Sixties Reader* (New York: Oxford University Press, 1995).

Leslie Brokaw, "The Dead Have Customers Too," *Inc.*, September, 1994: 90–92.

Jay Brown and R. McClen Novick, "An Interview with Jerry Garcia," *Magical Blend*, January 1994: 32–39; 88–89.

Jon Carroll, "Jerry Garcia by Jon Carroll," transcript of a 1982 interview, www.rkdn.org/Dead/Conversation.asp.

Patricia Cohen, "Innovation Far Removed from the Lab," *New York Times*, February 9, 2011.

Cone, 2007 Cone Cause Evolution Survey, www.market ingcharts.com/topics/branding/us-consumers-employees-want-socially-conscious-companies-912/.

Bernard Cova, Robert Kozinets, and Avi Shankar, eds., *Consumer Tribes* (Oxford, UK: Elsevier, 2007).

Cameron Crowe, "The Dead Show Off New Bodies," *Creem*, January 1974.

W. Edwards Deming, *Out of the Crisis* (Cambridge, Mass.: Massachusetts Institute of Technology, 1986).

David G. Dodd and Diana Spaulding, eds., *The Grateful Dead Reader* (New York: Oxford University Press, 2000).

Tom Dupree, "Grateful Dead: Hipper Than the Average Corporation," *Zoo World*, January 31, 1974: 12 13.

Editors of *Rolling Stone*, *Garcia* (New York: Little, Brown, 1995).

Benjy Eisen, "Rolling Stones Tour Manager Sam Cutler Finally Tells His Side of the Altamont Fiasco," *Spinner*, March 29, 2010, www .spinner.com/2010/03/29/sam-cutler-rolling-stones-altamont/.

David Gans, *Conversations with the Dead: The Grateful Dead Interview Book* (Cambridge, Mass.: Da Capo Press, 2002).

Jerry Garcia interview with Steve Marcus, October 14, 1986. Transcript courtesy Grateful Dead Productions and S. Marcus.

Jerry Garcia and Len Dell'Amico press appearance, October 12, 1987. Transcript courtesy Grateful Dead Productions.

Christopher Goodwin, "Think Different, Man!" *Sunday Times* (London), August 1, 2010.

Joshua Green, "Management Secrets of the Grateful Dead," *The Atlantic*, March 2010.

Robert Greenfield, *Dark Star: An Oral Biography of Jerry Garcia* (New York: William Morrow, 1996).

James Henke, "The Rolling Stone Interview: Jerry Garcia," *Rolling Stone* 616 (October 31, 1991): 34–40; 103–08.

Sam Hill and Glenn Rifkin, *Radical Marketing: From Harvard to Harley, Lessons from Ten That Broke the Rules and Made It Big* (New York: Harper Paperbacks, 2000).

Tony Hsieh, *Delivering Happiness: A Path to Profits, Passion, and Purpose* (New York: Business Plus, 2010).

Blair Jackson, *Garcia: An American Life* (New York: Viking, 1999).

Blair Jackson, *Grateful Dead Gear: The Band's Instruments, Sound Systems, and Recording Sessions from 1965 to 1995* (San Francisco: Backbeat Books, 2006).

Blair Jackson, "Garcia: An American Life: Outtakes, Afterthoughts and Other Cool Stuff," www.blairjackson.com.

Richard Kostelanetz, *The Theatre of Mixed Means* (New York: Dial Press, 1968).

"Phil Lesh: Operating Principles," JamBase, www.jambase.com/Articles/4909/PHIL-LESH-OPERATING-PRINCIPLES.

Phil Lesh, *Searching for the Sound: My Life with the Grateful Dead* (New York: Little, Brown, 2005).

Annie Lowrey, "Concerted Effort: The Dave Matthews Band Shows How to Make Money in the Music Industry," *Slate*, January 3, 2011, www.slate.com/id/2279757.

David Marsh, "Can the Dead Survive Putting Out Their Own Records?" *Newsday*, November 18, 1973.

Dennis McNally, *A Long Strange Trip: The Inside History of the Grateful Dead* (New York: Broadway Books, 2002).

Thomas V. Morris, *If Aristotle Ran General Motors: The New Soul of Business* (New York: Henry Holt and Company, 1997).

Steve Parish, "Dead to the World," interview with David Gans, September 24, 2003, thedeadbeat.com.

Craig L. Pearce and Jay A. Conger, eds., *Shared Leadership: Reframing the Hows and Whys of Leadership* (Thousand Oaks, Calif.: Sage Publications, 2003).

Thomas J. Peters and Robert H. Waterman, *In Search of Excellence: Lessons from America's Best-Run Companies* (New York: Harper & Row, 1982).

Frederick Reichheld with Thomas Teal, *The Loyalty Effect*, (Boston: Harvard Business School Press, 1996).

Glenn Rifkin, "How to 'Truck' the Brand: Lessons from the Grateful Dead," *Strategy + Business* 6, January 1, 1997.

Mary Scott and Howard Rothman, *Companies with a Conscience: In-Depth Profiles of Businesses that are Making a Difference* (Franklin Lakes, N.J.: Career, 2002).

David Shenk and Steve Silberman, *Skeleton Key: A Dictionary for Deadheads* (New York, Doubleday, 1994).

Jon Sievert, "Jerry Garcia: New Life with the Dead," *Guitar Player*, July 1988: 86–102.

Alan Trist, "A Balanced Objective: Overview of Job Definitions," internal Grateful Dead business document, June 1981.

John L. Wasserman, "The Expansion of the Grateful Dead," *San Francisco Chronicle*, October 12, 1973.

Robert G. Weiner, *Perspectives on the Grateful Dead: Critical Writings* (Westport, Conn.: Greenwood Press, 1999).

Index

**BUSINESS
PLUS**

Recognized as one of the world's most prestigious business imprints, Business Plus specializes in publishing books that are on the cutting edge. Like you, to be successful we always strive to be ahead of the curve.

Business Plus titles encompass a wide range of books and interests—including important business management works, state-of-the-art personal financial advice, noteworthy narrative accounts, the latest in sales and marketing advice, individualized career guidance, and autobiographies of the key business leaders of our time.

Our philosophy is that business is truly global in every way, and that today's business reader is looking for books that are both entertaining and educational. To find out more about what we're publishing, please check out the Business Plus blog at:

www.businessplusblog.com